Creating Homeowner

&

Condo Association

Documents

Creating Homeowner & Condo Association Documents

How to Protect Your HOA or Con-Dough

David I. Goldenberg, Ph.D.

A Condo Commandos 101 Reality Book
Publisher: Dr. Joyce Starr
Imprint: Little Guy Pawprint
www.Dr.JoyceStarr.com

Publisher: Dr. Joyce Starr, Adventura, FL USA

Imprint: Little Guy Pawprint

A Condo Commandos 101 Reality Book

www.DrJoyceStarr.com

Aventura, Florida

© 2006 by David I Goldenberg, Ph.D.   Boynton Beach, FL USA.
All Rights Reserved in All Media.

Published in the United States of America.

No part of this book may be used or reproduced in any manner whatsoever without written permission of the author, save for brief quotations embodied in articles or reviews and as permitted under Section 107 or Section 108 of the United States Copyright Act, without the prior permission of the publisher.

ISBN 978-0-9792333-8-8

This book is available for special promotions. Please contact: info@DrJoyceStarr.com

First Edition – 2007

Printed in the United States of America.

FROM THE PUBLISHER

Our small publishing house is designed to work closely with writers who have empowering and inspirational material to share.

Publishing is perceived as an impersonal process. Yet the publisher and senior editor often have more intense contact with the author and a deeper involvement in the author's project than most readers.

Author David Goldenberg takes an empowering view of the rules and rulers governing Home Owner Associations (HOAs) and condos. He asserts that just as there are good and bad rules and rulers, both are subject to change. What matters is knowledge of and conformity to fair and consistent rules. Problems arise when bad or obsolete rules are enforced or good rules are either ignored or ineptly enforced. Foresight, experience and tact prevent such problems.

Utopia, for example, is currently a no-pet community. But that's a starting point—and definitely not one of the Ten Commandments. Owners and board members alike must learn the rules and proper ways to modify outdated rules. Goldenberg shows them how to change or enforce their community's rules and rulers. As one who believes that no-pet bylaws and rules should be subject to change, I'm especially happy to report that Dave's next work will offer suggestions for modifying or eliminating especially contentious issues, including pet-friendly provisions.

Now for a word about Dave: He's an inspiration. Incredibly accomplished, knowledgeable, witty and kind. Ready to help at every turn. It was a privilege to publish his book and a pleasure to encounter such a remarkable individual.

DISCLAIMER

This document was not prepared by an attorney. It is, however, based on legal documents in current use. This document is not intended as a substitute for an attorney's advice. Legal advice almost certainly would be essential since complex matters of real property, contract and constitutional law are at issue and their interpretation varies across state jurisdictions and over time.

This document shows owners of residences in homeowner and/or condominium associations how they can protect their rights, especially the right to peaceful enjoyment of their property, against disruptive behavior by other parties particularly aggressive, self-aggrandizing, inept, self-serving or vicious directors, attorneys for the board, management service firms, developers and so forth by revising their community's governing documents. This document adapted principles and techniques from regulatory economics and game theory to achieve a desirable goal focus as well as clarity and objective measurement by slightly modifying conventional governing documents of homeowner and/or condominium associations.

The publisher and the author used their best efforts in preparing this book. Nevertheless, they make no representation or warranties as to the accuracy or completeness of the contents of this book. They also specifically disclaim any implied warranties of merchantability or fitness for a particular purpose. No warranty may be created or extended by sales representatives or written sales materials. The advice and strategies contained herein may not be suitable for your situation. Moreover, the publisher is not engaged in providing professional service so you should consult with a professional where appropriate. Neither the publisher nor the author shall be liable for any loss of profit or any other commercial damages, including but not limited to special, consequential or other damages.

ACKNOWLEDGMENTS

The author acknowledges adapting the AARP's proposed model statutes for use in governing documents of Homeowner and Condominium Associations.

The author particularly wishes to thank a group of homeowners best left unidentified. Their behavior over a period of years inspired and guided the development of these documents. That anonymous group's good and bad examples deserve recognition and thanks.

The author also wishes to extend appreciation to publisher and editor Dr. Joyce Starr for untold hours transforming my manuscript into an effective and cohesive message, preparing it for publication and creating a final cover design. Thank you for your enthusiasm and for so encouraging, patient and congenial an attitude.

Finally, the author thanks graphics artists Jonathan D. and Polette Villalta for rendering such powerful cover artwork.

DEDICATION

This book is dedicated to Ellie, Mrs. Elinor A. Goldenberg, for 50 years of shared love and laughter. She deserves the best anyone can offer and certainly more than that from this admiring and devoted husband.

PREFACE

Illyrian Dales Master Association, Utopia Homes — a Homeowners Association [HOA], and Conch County are aliases for real organizations in Florida. However, the very problems facing these fictional entities are based on the actual experiences of similar entities throughout the country.

Serious recurring problems plague homeowner and condominium associations throughout the United States. These usually are addressed on a case-by-case basis. That is a costly and slow process with a poor and mutually unsatisfactory record of success for all but the attorneys involved. The governing documents proposed below offer a new approach to permanently eliminate most of those problems and moderate the rest by dealing with the causes of the problems rather than the individual disruptions arising from those causes.

Potent and frequent causes of HOA problems include:

1. old, vague, incomplete, governing documents written in hard to understand "legalese";
2. vague, incomplete, badly drawn laws which are neither enforced nor enforceable;
3. conflicts of interest between attorneys, developers, HOA boards, homeowners, insurers, legislators, and/or management service firms which typically are resolved at the expense of homeowner interests;
4. ignorance of the laws, governing documents and proper procedure by HOA boards and/or homeowners;
5. apathetic HOA boards and/or homeowners;
6. incompetent and/or self-serving HOA boards;
7. unintentional as well as deliberate abuse of power by HOA boards;
8. persistent violation of the laws and/or governing documents by "troublemakers";
9. stubbornness or unwillingness to compromise;
10. inability or reluctance to deal with violations promptly and effectively;

11. imposition of changes desired by a few activists without approval of the majority; and
12. a community too small to reliably supply competent directors.

The recommended new approach involves updating your homeowner association's governing documents along the lines indicated in the sample documents below. Those documents were designed to prevent the known causes of problems from taking effect. A number of different devices were introduced to accomplish this goal. Some of those devices are novel in the related areas of law although accepted in other fields of law. For example, there is an objective way to measure the intensity of a conflict of interest — The Lorenz-Gini Coefficient. That allows a community to limit the amount of conflict of interest it will tolerate among its directors. Other devices: limit the board's power to its primary areas of responsibility; subordinate the board to the will of the community; set explicit definitions, standards and procedures to follow; establish objective and enforceable eligibility and performance criteria for service on a board; and promptly reward proper and effective behavior of directors and residents while quickly penalizing improper and/or ineffective behavior. Perhaps the largest and most notable improvement is the near wholesale adaptation of the model statutes proposed by the American Association of Retired People [AARP]. AARP hopes to eventually have its 10 proposed statutes adopted nationally. That, however, will take many years. It's also virtually certain the legislative process will distort and weaken those proposals in different ways in each state. Fortunately, a homeowners association can quickly incorporate at least nine of AARP's 10 model statutes in its governing documents. Unfortunately, a community cannot enact AARP's tenth proposed statute to create an effective ombudsman. Only a legislature can do that. But one need not wait on federal or state legislative action to put the rest of AARP's model statutes into effect in your community.

A community considering adopting these documents must first adapt them to its circumstances. Then it should win the approval of its members for that revision. Finally, it should tell its attorney to "make it legal." For example, Utopia is a no-pet community. Alternatively, one might either allow any kind of pet, regardless of its size or nature, or restrict pets in one or more ways. Indoor pets might be allowed but not outdoor pets. Small pets might be allowed but not large ones by limiting pets to species where the typical adult weighs less X pounds. Similarly, Utopia has carports rather than parking spaces or garages. The key point is to have clear, objective and complete standards and to make sure they are widely and regularly communicated to all and also are enforceable and enforced.

Our basic point is that homeowners have rights and are entitled to have those preserved and enforced rather than ignored or abused. If you're considering moving into a homeowners association, make sure that its governing documents protect your rights at least as well as those below would. If you're already living in a homeowners association with weaker governing documents, upgrade them. It's the best investment in personal freedom and harmony that you'll ever make.

The documents recommended below apply to condominiums too. As the relevant laws for condominiums are somewhat different, some further, but not difficult, adjustments are needed. Any competent and experienced attorney should be able to make the necessary adaptations in a few hours.

You and your neighbors are entitled to decide how you want to live. Without rules all of you will suffer under anarchy. With bad rules / rulers all of you will suffer under tyranny. Only with good rules and rulers is there harmony. It's up to you and your neighbors to set good rules and pick good rulers. Choose wisely. The price of a mistake is lasting anarchy or tyranny.

TABLE OF CONTENTS

STATEMENT OF DISCLOSURE 1

DECLARATION OF MAINTENANCE COVENANTS 7

Article 1. Definitions 7
    Section 1. Definitions Adapted from
                 IDMA's Declaration   7
    Section 2. Definitions of Key Terms   13

Article 2. Property Subject to this Utopia Declaration 17

Article 3. Plan of Operation 17
    Section 1. Use of Common Area   17
    Section 2. Rules for the Common Area   18
    Section 3. Types of Land in Utopia   18
    Section 4. Operational Priorities   20
    Section 5. Policy Guidelines   24
    Section 6. Key Premise and Interpretation   25
    Section 7. Incorporation of IDMA and Utopia   26

Article 4. Property Rights, Easements and Restrictions 27
    Section 1. Title to Utopia Exclusive Common Area   27
    Section 2. Obligations of Members; Remedies; ...   27
    Section 3. Easements of Enjoyment   29
    Section 4. Easements for Building Encroachment
                 and Common Structural Elements   30
    Section 5. Reservation of Right to Grant Easements
                 and Licenses   31
    Section 6. Restrictions on Dwelling Unit Leases   31
    Section 7. Restrictions on Dwelling Unit Sales   32
    Section 8. Enforceability of Certain Covenants   34
    Section 9. General FHLMC Requirements   34
    Section 10. FHLMC Insurance Requirements   39
    Section 11. Other FHLMC Requirements   40
    Section 12. Prospective Purchasers`   41

Article 5. Requirements for Contracts and Bids 41
    Section 1. Relevant Contracts   41
    Section 2. Exceptions   42

Section 3. Contracts with Community Management
firms 42
Section 4. Contractor Standards 43

Article 6. Utopia Property Owners Association, Inc. 43
Section 1. Not-for-profit Corporation 43
Section 2. Intervention by IDMA 43
Section 3. Directors are Fiduciaries of Members 44
Section 4. Legal Actions 45

Article 7. Maintenance and Repair Obligations 45
Section 1. General 45
Section 2. Damage Caused by an Owner, Tenant,
Guest, etc. 46

Article 8. Covenants for Assessments 47
Section 1. Creation of the Lien and Personal
Obligation for the Assessment 47
Section 2. Purpose of Assessments 47
Section 3. CAP on Improvements 48
Section 4. CAP on Attorney's Fees 48
Section 5. Annual Assessment 50
Section 6. Special Assessments 50
Section 7. Apportionment of Assessments 50
Section 8. Status of Assessments 51
Section 9. Effect of and Remedies for
Nonpayment of Assessments 51
Section 10. Subordination of the Lien to Mortgages 51
Section 11. Exempt Property 52
Section 12. Termination of Assessment Liens 52
Section 13. Two-year Assessments and Capped
as to Increases 53

Article 9. General Provisions , ... 53
Section 1. Duration 53
Section 2. Notices 54
Section 3. Dispute Resolution 54
Section 4. Enforcement 59
Section 5. Severability 60
Section 6. Subdivision Use Restrictions 60
Section 7. Effective Date 60
Section 8. Amendments 60

Section 9. Prohibited Clauses in These
                Governing Documents   61
Section 10. Right of Security against Foreclosure   64
Section 11. Right to Fairness in Litigation   66
Section 12. Right to Be Told of All Rules and Charges   67
Section 13. Right to Stability in Rules and Charges   70
Section 14. Right to Individual Autonomy   80
Section 15. Right to Oversight of the Association
                and Directors   78
Section 16. Right to Vote and Run for Office   85
Section 17. Right to Reasonable Association
                and Directors   88
Section 18. Declaration of Covenants: Survival
                after Tax Deed on Foreclosure   91
Section 19. Pets   91
Section 20. Pool Rules   92
Section 21. Rules for Working at or from Home
                in Utopia   96
Section 22. General Principles for All Meetings   97

ARTICLES OF INCORPORATION 101

Article 1. Name 101

Article 2. Purposes 101
    Section 1. Promote Property Owners' Health, Safety
               and Social Welfare   101
    Section 2. Hold Title to Common Areas   102
    Section 3. Maintenance and Repair   102
    Section 4. Architectural Control   102
    Section 5. Insure Compliance with Master Land
              Use Plan   102
    Section 6. Other   102
    Section 7. A Nonprofit Operation Solely for
               Member's Benefit   103
    Section 8. Subject to IDMA's Declaration and
               Enforcement of It in Utopia   103

Article 3. General Powers 103

Article 4. Members 105
   Section 1. Link Between Lot Owners and UPOAI
           Members   105
   Section 2. SLAPP Lawsuits Barred   105

Article 5. Voting 106
   Section 1. Basic Vote   106
   Section 2. Earned Votes   107
   Section 3. Notice   107
   Section 4. Use of an Agent   108
   Section 5. Voting   108
   Section 6. Ballots   108
   Section 7. Vote Counting   108
   Section 8. Penalty for Not Voting   109
   Section 9. Funding Restriction   109

Article 6. Assessments 109
   Section 1. General   109
   Section 2. Restrictions on Assessments   110

Article 7. Reserves 112
   Section 1. General   112
   Section 2. Commingling   112
   Section 3. Diversion   112
   Section 4. Funding of Reserves   112
   Section 5. Purposes   112
   Section 6. Trees and Reserves   113
   Section 7. Target Size and Time to Target   113

Article 8. Board of Directors 114
   Section 1. Board of Directors as the Association's
           Administrative Body   114
   Section 2. Staggered Terms   115
   Section 3. Recall   115
   Section 4. Resignations   116
   Section 5. Suspension   116
   Section 6. Board Meetings   119
   Section 7. Receivership   122
   Section 8. Minutes Required   123
   Section 9. Prohibitions   123

Article 9. Officers 124
    Section 1. Association Administered by Officers   124
    Section 2. Election of Officers   124
    Section 3. Fiduciary Standards   124
    Section 4. Signatory Authority   125

Article 10. Corporate Existence 125

Article 11. Bylaws 125

Article 12. Amendment to the Articles of Incorporation 126

Article 13. Indemnification 126
    Section 1. Commitment to Indemnify   126
    Section 2. Association's Power to Indemnify   127

Article 14. Conflict of Interest 128
    Section 1. General   128
    Section 2. Effect of a Conflict of Interest on a Quorum   128

Article 15. Dissolution of the Association 128
    Section 1. Real Property   128
    Section 2. Personal Property   129

Article 16. Definitions 129

BYLAWS OF UTOPIA POA, INC. 131

Article 1. Definitions 131
    Section 1. Referral to Declaration   131
    Section 2. Subordination   131

Article 2. Location of Principal Office 131

Article 3. Board Meetings; Notice, Proxies; Assessments ... 132
    Section 1. Meetings   132
    Section 2. Meeting Notices   132
    Section 3. Assessment Notice   133
    Section 4. Voting by Directors   133

Article 4. Members 134
    Section 1. Quorum; Amendments   134
    Section 2. Annual Meeting   134
    Section 3. Special Meetings   135

Section 4. Notice of Meetings 136
Section 5. Right to Speak 136
Section 6. Adjournment 136
Section 7. Proxy Voting by Members 137
Section 8. Elections 138
Section 9. Nominations for Directors 138
Section 10. Eligibility for Board Service 139
Section 11. Recording 140
Section 12. Record Date 140

Article 5. Directors 140
   Section 1. Board of Director's Authority and
              Qualifications for Directorships 140
   Section 2. Board Meetings 141
   Section 3. Service of Meeting Notices 141
   Section 4. Members as Observers; Right to Speak 142
   Section 5. Voting by Directors 142
   Section 6. Filling Board Vacancies 142
   Section 7. Waiver of Notice 143
   Section 8. Quorum 143
   Section 9. Executive Committee 143
   Section 10. Exercise of Board's Powers and Duties 143
   Section 11. Nepotism 145

Article 6. Officers 145
   Section 1. List 145
   Section 2. Election 146
   Section 3. Officer's Duties and Powers 146
   Section 4. Delegation of Officer's Duties 149

Article 7. Committees 150
   Section 1. Standing Committees 150

   Section 2. Powers and Duties of the Grounds
              Maintenance Control Committee 152
   Section 3. Architectural Control Committee 152
   Section 4. Composition, Powers and Duties of
              the Nominating Committee 158
   Section 5. Ad Hoc Committees 160

xviii

Article 8. Budgets and Financial Reporting 162
    Section 1. Budgets   162
    Section 2. Financial Reporting   163

Article 9. Official Records 164
    Section 1. Documents to be Retained   164
    Section 2. Access to Association Records   165

Article 10. Seal 167

Article 11. Amendments 167
    Section 1. Sources of Amendment   167
    Section 2. Notice of Proposed Amendment   167
    Section 3. Approval of Proposed Amendment 168
    Section 4. Certification of Amendment(s)   168
    Section 5. Amendments and Mortgagees   169

Article 12. Prior Resolutions and/or Motions 169
    Section 1. Continuity of Board's Motions and/or
                Resolutions   169
    Section 2. Motions and/or Resolutions in Effect   169

INDEX 171

STATEMENT OF DISCLOSURE

FOR

UTOPIA HOMES AT ILLYRIAN DALES

OWNING A DWELLING IN UTOPIA MEANS THAT YOU HAVE AGREED TO OBEY THE RULES SET FORTH IN THESE GOVERNING DOCUMENTS EVEN IF YOU HAVE NOT READ OR UNDERSTOOD THEM.

READ THESE DOCUMENTS CAREFULLY OR HAVE YOUR ATTORNEY DO SO AND BRIEF YOU BEFORE BUYING A RESIDENCE IN UTOPIA. ASK YOUR ATTORNEY IF YOU'VE ANY QUESTIONS ABOUT YOUR RIGHTS AND DUTIES AS A UTOPIA HOMEOWNER.

THIS STATEMENT OF DISCLOSURE IS NOT INTENDED TO BE A SUBSTITUTE FOR THE READING OF EACH DOCUMENT.

BEFORE BUYING OR SELLING A DWELLING IN UTOPIA, IT IS YOUR RESPONSIBILITY TO READ AND UNDERSTAND THIS STATEMENT OF DISCLOSURE AND THE THREE GOVERNING DOCUMENTS IT SUMMARIZES. THOSE GOVERNING DOCUMENTS ARE: THE DECLARATION OF MAINTENANCE COVENANTS, THE ARTICLES OF INCORPORATION AND THE BYLAWS. THOSE THREE DOCUMENTS STATE THE LEGALLY BINDING AND LEGALLY ENFORCEABLE RULES GOVERNING ALL UTOPIA PROPERTY OWNERS AS WELL AS THE UTOPIA PROPERTY OWNERS ASSOCIATION, INC. THOSE RULES SIGNIFICANTLY AFFECT THE USE, SALABILITY AND VALUE OF DWELLINGS IN UTOPIA. YOUR RESPONSIBILITY TO READ, UNDERSTAND AND FOLLOW THE RULES SET FORTH IN THE GOVERNING DOCUMENTS EXTENDS TO SEEING THAT YOUR LESSEES, GUESTS AND INVITEES DO THE SAME. For example, there are penalties, including fines, if you allow a live pet into your home or if you alter either the exterior of your home or the ground around it without prior written authorization from the Architectural Control Committees of Utopia and IDMA or if you try to do certain types of work at home.

Illyrian Dales

Illyrian Dales contains approximately 761 acres. The Common Areas presently include waterways, roadways, paths, and open space. However, the members-only country club is not part of Illyrian Dales' common area.

The Master Plan includes separate, homogeneous subdivisions or neighborhoods within the development. In addition to the Common Areas available for the use of all Illyrian Dales residents, each subdivision has its own exclusive Common Area and facilities.

The development and operations of Illyrian Dales are governed by the provisions of (1) the Declaration of Maintenance Covenants for Illyrian Dales, (2) the Restrictions for Illyrian Dales, and (3) the Restrictive Covenant. These documents refer to Illyrian Dales Master Association, Inc. [IDMA], a Florida corporation not-for-profit, which holds title to certain of the Common Areas and is the entity ultimately responsible for ensuring conformity with the Master Plan, and the enforcement of all covenants and restrictions relating to Illyrian Dales.

The IDMA has the responsibility of collecting funds from the owners of parcels at Illyrian Dales for the funding of its operations. This function is performed by IDMA's Board of Directors, which levies an assessment against the dwelling units and their owners. If the assessment is not paid, the Association's lien for unpaid assessments may be foreclosed.

The Declaration and the Restrictions expire, respectively, on March 29, 2051 and December 17, 2050. They are renewable, under certain circumstances, for successive periods of ten (10) years each.

Utopia

Utopia is a platted subdivision containing approximately 15.2 acres at Illyrian Dales. There are 23 Blocks on which a total of 92 one-story single-family dwelling units were built. The remaining land is described as the Common Area.

The Utopia Recreation Area contains .4 acres in the Exclusive Common Area with a swimming pool, a bathhouse and a pool deck.

Utopia POA, Inc. is the Florida corporation not-for-profit serving as a vehicle to own and manage the Exclusive Common Area at Utopia. Some of its purposes, duties and responsibilities include:

A) To own, manage, repair and replace the Common Area property such as the paved paths to the pool, the sidewalk on the north side of the island encircled by Utopia Drive, and Utopia Drive [the road];

B) To exercise architectural control of the improvements at Utopia so as to keep exteriors, including walls and roofs, in conformity with their original design, materials and colors;

C) To maintain and repair the exterior surface of stucco walls, fascia and/or soffits of dwelling units, as well as the yards, driveways, sprinkler systems and landscaping of the Lots, [Exterior does not refer to either the structural interior of such walls or a unit's roof], the Utopia Property Owners Association, Inc. can increase maintenance fees to establish a reserve fund to pay for periodic power washing of the roofs, gutters, sidewalks and driveways as well as periodic painting of the exterior walls [but not the roofs] of those dwelling units needing such service(s) and may charge the owners for such costs;

D) To assess the owners of dwelling units for the cost and expense of its administration, and

E) To enforce the covenants and restrictions relating to Utopia.

All owners of dwelling units at Utopia are members of the Utopia POA, Inc. [UPOAI] Its Board of Directors has the responsibility to levy assessments against the dwelling units and their owners as a source of funds to carry out its responsibilities. The Board may also levy an assessment against a specific dwelling unit and its owner when the owner has caused damage to any of the property under the control of UPOAI. At the time of levying an assessment, a lien is created in favor of the Property Owners Association against the dwelling unit. The governing documents explain in detail how both the Utopia POA, Inc. and its Board of Directors must act or refrain from acting in carrying out their responsibilities. The same documents also explain how the Members must act or refrain from acting in carrying out the responsibilities they accepted to join the community. Those rules protect Member's rights and privileges as much as possible while limiting them as little as possible and yet assure that Utopia POAI has sufficient authority to meet its duties and obligations to the Members. These detailed rules promote harmony within Utopia by encouraging, and if necessary compelling, all parties to make informed and deliberate decisions, act in the best long-term interests of the overall community, and assuring that any changes to the contractual relations established in the governing documents are made with the full knowledge and consent of the majority of the homeowners, are feasible and likely to generate the net benefits advanced as justifying such changes, and that those benefits are as evenly distributed across the homeowners as desired and practical.

If an assessment is not paid within thirty (30) days after it is due, an action may be brought to legally file a lien against the parcel. The costs of such action, and interest, may be added to any judgment which is obtained.

The Associations' Budgets

Illyrian Dales Maintenance Association, Inc. and Utopia Property Owners Association, Inc. [UPOAI] prepare budgets which are estimates of their anticipated expenses and revenues. These budgets form the basis for setting maintenance fees and assessments.

No representation or warranty can be made by Illyrian Dales Master Association, Inc. and/or Utopia Property Owners Association, Inc. that assessments will not increase in the future. The Utopia Property Owners Association will be governed by the Owners. Its Board of Directors will then estimate the anticipated expenses and levy maintenance fees and assessments accordingly.

COMPLETENESS OF THIS STATEMENT

AS STATED ABOVE, THE PURPOSE OF THIS STATEMENT IS TO SET FORTH A SUMMARY OF THE DOCUMENTS GOVERNING UTOPIA'S OPERATIONS. EACH PROSPECTIVE PURCHASER SHOULD REFER TO THE ACTUAL DOCUMENTS FOR THE COMPLETE AND SPECIFIC TERMS AND PROVISIONS CONTAINED THEREIN AS YOU WILL BE LEGALLY BOUND BY THOSE TERMS AND PROVISIONS ON PURCHASING A DWELLING IN UTOPIA.

The attached governing documents inherently are incomplete in certain important respects.

First, they are subordinate to various federal and state statutes and court decisions. Currently relevant statutes include, but are not limited to: the Federal Home Loan Mortgage Act, the Fair Debt Collection Practices Act [US Code Title 15], the Florida Consumer Collection Practices Act [Florida Statute 559], the Florida Homestead Act, the Florida Homeowners Association Act [FS 720], Corporation, Not for Profit [FS 617], the Florida Administrative Code, and various laws, ordinances and regulations of Conch County. However, the American Disability Act does not apply to Utopia.

Second, the applicable statutes and case law involve technical aspects and interactions of such fields of law as contract law, constitutional laws, corporate law and real property law. These interactions are complex and unsettled until resolved by an appellate court.

Third, those statutes, case law and decisions by the Board of Directors and the Members of Utopia's Property Owners' Association are subject to change with the passage of time.

Finally, the laws, case decisions, governing documents and changes to the latter constitute a dynamic hierarchy which requires training and experience to interpret correctly. Case decisions generally take precedence over the statutes but those laws take precedence over the Declaration of Maintenance Covenants which, in turn, takes precedence over the Articles of Incorporation and the Bylaws while the Articles of Incorporation take precedence over the Bylaws.

DECLARATION OF MAINTENANCE

COVENANTS FOR

UTOPIA HOMES AT ILLYRIAN DALES

THIS UTOPIA DECLARATION was reviewed and approved as of {insert an appropriate date} by the Utopia Property Owners Association, Inc. and supersedes all prior declarations of maintenance covenants. Utopia Property Owners Association, Inc. is a Florida corporation and the owner of all the real property described in Appendix "A" which is attached hereto, for the purpose of subjecting that real property to the following terms, conditions and covenants.

ARTICLE 1

Definitions

Section 1. Definitions Adapted from IDMA's Declaration. -- The following words, when used in this Utopia Declaration (unless the context shall prohibit), shall have the meanings ascribed to them in the Declaration of Maintenance Covenants for Illyrian Dales ("Illyrian Dales Declaration"). The definitions listed below have been adapted from the Illyrian Dales Declaration. If there are any discrepancies or inconsistencies, the definitions contained in the Illyrian Dales Declaration shall control unless superseded by statute or case law.

A) "Assessment" or "amenity fee" means a sum or sums of money payable to the Association or other owner of common areas, or to recreational facilities and other properties serving the parcels by the owners of one or more parcels as authorized in the governing documents, which if not paid by the owner of a parcel, can result in a lien against the parcel.

B) "Association" or "Homeowners' association" means a Florida corporation responsible for the operation of a community in which voting membership is made up of parcel owners or their agents, or a combination thereof, and in which membership is a mandatory condition of parcel ownership, and which is authorized to impose assessments that, if unpaid, may become a lien on the parcel. The term "homeowners' association" does not include a community development district or other similar special taxing district created pursuant to statute.

- 1) "Association" shall mean and refer to Illyrian Dales Master Association, Inc. [IDMA], a Florida corporation not for profit, its Articles of Incorporation and Bylaws.

- 2) The Utopia "Property Owners Association, Inc. [UPOAI] shall mean and refer to a Florida corporation, not-for-profit, for the purpose of making available to the Owners of lands in such particular tract certain recreational facilities and Common Areas.

C) "Common area" or common ground means all real property within a community which is owned or leased by an association or dedicated for use or maintenance by the association or its members, including, regardless of whether title has been conveyed to the association:

- 1) Real property the use of which is dedicated to the association or its members by plat; or
- 2) Real property committed by a declaration of covenants to be leased or conveyed to the association.
- 3) "Total Common Area" shall mean and refer to all the real property in Illyrian Dales conveyed or committed by Developers, pursuant to Article III, Section 1 of the Illyrian Dales Declaration to the Utopia Property Owners Association, Inc. for the exclusive or nonexclusive use of Owners.

4) "Exclusive Common Area" shall mean and refer to any Common Area which has been conveyed or committed pursuant to Article III, Section 1 of the Illyrian Dales Declaration to a Property Owners Association for the exclusive use of Owners of Parcels within that tract of land over which such Property Owners Association has jurisdiction.

5) "Common Area" shall mean and refer to some portion of the Total Common Area.

D) "Community" means the real property that is or will be subject to a declaration of covenants which is recorded in the county where the property is located. The term "community" includes all real property, including undeveloped phases, that is or was the subject of a development-of-regional-impact development order, together with any approved modification thereto.

E) "Declaration of covenants" or "declaration" means a recorded written instrument in the nature of covenants running with the land which subjects the land comprising the community to the jurisdiction and control of an association or associations in which the owners of the parcels, or their association representatives, must be members.

F) "Department" means the Department of Business and Professional Regulation [DBPR]

G) "Division" means the Division of Florida Land Sales, Condominiums, and Mobile Homes in the DBPR.

H) "Fiduciary duty" means and refers to the legal requirement imposing extremely high standards of responsibility and rational behavior on those serving as corporate officers, directors and/or committee members so that those individuals can be trusted to consistently put the overall community's interests far ahead of their own interests or those of their relatives, friends or business associates. An inability, reluctance, refusal or repeated failure to consistently satisfy the standards required of a fiduciary automatically and permanently disqualifies one from serving as a director or officer. The minimum behavioral standards required of a fiduciary are:

1) Putting the long-term best interests of the majority of the owners ahead of all other considerations including their own or those of other individual directors and/or officers as well as their relatives, friends or business colleagues. To that end, directors and officers are required disregard any and all emotional considerations, impacts on the financial condition of their family, friends or colleagues and personal preferences when discussing and voting on board matters.

2) Knowing the relevant laws and governing documents and also obeying them by acting solely and consistently in reliance on the letter and spirit of those documents and laws.

3) Refraining from trying to bypass, circumvent, evade, ignore, misrepresent, negate, pettifog, simplify, skirt, or weaken the relevant laws and governing documents and the definitions and procedures set forth in those documents.

4) Actively insisting that their peers behave appropriately as indicated in items 1), 2) and 3) above or insist on their immediate resignations.

l) "Governing documents" shall mean and refer to:

1) The recorded Declaration of Covenants for a community, and all adopted and recorded amendments, supplements, and recorded exhibits thereto; and

2) The recorded Articles of Incorporation and Bylaws of the homeowners' association and any duly adopted amendments thereto.

J) "Illyrian Dales" shall mean and refer to the real property described in Exhibit "A" of the Illyrian Dales Declaration, together with any additions made pursuant to Article II, Section 1 thereof.

K) "Maintenance" shall mean and refer to periodic preventive measures intended to keep common ground and exteriors of dwellings in proper working condition according to original designs of the community or approved alterations to those designs. Examples of maintenance include regular cutting of grass on common ground, power washing, painting, lubrication of motors and pumps, and so forth. Maintenance activities are complemented by repairs (see below).

L) "Master Plan" shall mean and refer to that certain land use plan for Illyrian Dales on file with Conch County, Florida, pursuant to its Planned Unit Development Ordinance.

M) "Member" means a Member of an association, and may include, but is not limited to, a parcel owner or an association representing parcel owners or a combination thereof, and includes any person or entity obligated by the governing documents to pay an assessment or amenity fee.

N) "Owner" shall mean and refer to the record fee simple title holder, whether one or more persons or entities, of a Parcel.

O) "Parcel" means a platted or unplatted lot, tract, unit or other subdivision of real property within a community, as described in the declaration:

    1) Which is capable of separate conveyance; and
    2) Of which the parcel owner, or an association in which the parcel owner must be a member is obligated:

[a] By the governing documents to be a member of an association that serves the community; and
[b] To pay the homeowners' association assessments that, if not paid, may result in a lien.

P) "Parcel owner" means the record owner(s) of legal title to a parcel.

Q) "Proxy" has two distinct but related meanings with the appropriate one a matter of context. One definition of a proxy means and refers to an individual authorized to act as an agent, either as specifically directed or according to his judgment — that is, with discretion, for a principal in all or some way(s) that said principal could do if the latter chose to act personally or was able to do. Alternatively, a proxy means and refers to a document which authorizes a designated individual to act as an agent for the principal provided that document meets certain legal requirements as to form and content.

R) "Repair(s)" shall mean and refer to those irregular activities intended to restore common ground to normal operation or as close as possible to its condition. Repairs typically involve fixing or replacing something broken either as a result of wear and tear in the course of normal operations or an outside force such as a lighting bolt or a storm. Repair activities may involve replacing all or part of a piece of equipment, such as a motor bearing or an entire motor, or a part or all of structure on or in common ground, such as a sprinkler head or roof. Repairs complement maintenance activities and may be interpreted as synonymous with them.

S) "Voting interest" means the voting rights distributed to the members of the homeowners' association pursuant to the governing documents.

Section 2. Definitions of Key Terms. - - The following words, when used in this Utopia Declaration (unless the context shall prohibit), shall have the meaning ascribed below:

A) "Association" shall mean and refer to an organization, including homeowners as members, created to manage the property or affairs of a common-interest community.

B) "Common interest community" shall mean and refer to a real-estate development or neighborhood in which individually owned lots or units are burdened by a servitude that imposes and obligation that cannot be avoided by nonuse or withdrawal:

1) to pay for the use of, or contribute to the maintenance of, property held or enjoyed in common by the individual owners, or to pay dues or assessments to an association that provides services or facilities to the common property or to the individually owned property, or

2) to pay dues or assessments to an association that provides services or facilities to the common property or to the individually owned property, or that enforces other servitudes burdening the property in the development or neighborhood

C) "Common property" shall mean and refer to property rights of an identical or a similar kind held by the homeowners as appurtenances to their individually owned lots or units.

D) "Common Structural Elements" shall mean and refer to the following portions of dwelling units (with or without their attached carports) the flooring, party walls and roofing. "Common Structural Elements" are not the same as "Common Community Property" or "Common Grounds." Roofs on multiplex dwellings may be a common structural element but are not common community property.

E) "Declaration" shall mean and refer to the recorded document or documents containing the servitudes that create and govern the common-interest community.

F) "Directors" shall mean and refer to the persons who constitute the Association's senior administrative body, in articles of incorporation or articles of association, or in other governing documents.

G) A "dwelling unit" or "unit" shall mean and refer to a single family residence on a lot in Utopia which is part of a multiplex building.

H) "Emergency" shall mean and refer to any situation which could not have been reasonably foreseen, poses a significant and immediate threat to the community, and makes compliance with many provisions of these governing documents, particularly those concerning scheduling, giving notice for, and/or holding Board, Board committee and/or Members meetings, impractical.

I) "Utopia Homes" shall mean and refer to the name given to the plat of Tract I according to the Master Plan for Illyrian Dales. The legal description of Tract I is described in Exhibit "A" attached hereto and may also be called "Utopia".

J) "Utopia Plat" shall mean and refer to the plat of Utopia, which plat was filed in the Official Records of Conch county, Utopia, and which consists of Common Areas and twenty-three (23) consecutively lettered Blocks, each of which was subdivided into four lots.

K) "Utopia POA, Inc." shall mean and refer to the Utopia corporation, not for profit, which is the Property Owners Association for the Utopia Parcel.

L) "Utopia Board" shall mean and refer to the Board of Directors of the Utopia Property Owners Association.

M) "Utopia Documents" shall mean and refer to this Declaration of Maintenance Covenants, the Articles of Incorporation and Bylaws of Utopia POA, Inc., and all of the instruments and documents referred to therein.

N) "Governing documents" shall mean and refer to the declaration and other documents, such as the articles of incorporation or articles of association, bylaws, architectural guidelines, and rules and regulations that determine rights or obligations of homeowners or that otherwise govern the management or operation of an association.

O) "Homeowner" shall mean the owner of property burdened by a servitude described in the definition above of a common-interest community.

P) Improvement or capital improvement shall mean and refer to an alteration, regardless of its monetary cost, to some or all of Utopia's common ground or commonly owned structure(s) which takes at least eight (8) man-hours to implement, is not obviously and completely a maintenance and/or repair matter, and has potentially long-lasting consequences. The alteration(s) in question also does one or more of the following: increase or decrease the amount of common property; changes to any degree the character, color, durability, nature, quality, size, or use patterns of the common ground or structure; or creates, alters or terminates a financial arrangement involving the common ground or structure(s) thereon.

Q) "Lot" shall mean and refer to any one of the Parcels into which Blocks of the Utopia Plat are divided, and there shall be no more than one single family unit on each Lot.

R) "Multiplex Building" shall mean and refer to a building constructed and existing entirely within the boundaries of one of the twenty-three (23) consecutively lettered Blocks of Utopia Plat and containing four dwelling units, each of which is:

1) attached to each adjoining dwelling unit by party walls with no portion of any dwelling unit extending into the space below or above any other dwelling unit, and

2) constructed and existing entirely within the boundaries of one of the Lots into which the Block has been subdivided by a Plat thereof to be filed for record; provided, however, that the existence of any encroachments shall not preclude a building meeting the above definitions from being a Multiplex Building.

S) "Notice" shall mean and refer to, with respect to any person, sending regular and certified mail (return receipt requested) to the person's last known address. For homeowners, it means each address where the Association sends its annual assessments, written in plain English, dated and signed by an officer of UPOAI.

T) "Operating rule" shall mean and refer to any rule or regulation not stated in the governing documents whether adopted by the Directors or by homeowners in a vote, that applies to the management or operation of the Association or to the conduct of the business and affairs of the Association, including (without limitation) user fees, charges for any violations of the governing documents of the Association, and other fees or charges.

U) "Party Wall" shall mean and refer to a vertical wall common to adjoining dwelling units and centered on the boundary line between the Lots on which the said adjoining dwelling units are constructed and existing; provided, however, that the existence of any encroachment shall not preclude a wall, meeting the above definition, from being a Party Wall.

V) "Rule change" shall mean and refer to adoption, amendment, or repeal of an operating rule.

W) "Servitude" shall mean and refer to a restriction on or limitation of behavior.

ARTICLE 2

Property Subject to this Utopia Declaration

The real property which is and shall be held, transferred, sold, conveyed and occupied subject to this Utopia Declaration is located in Conch county, Utopia, and is legally described in Appendix "A"; all of said real property shall hereinafter be referred to as "Utopia" and is subject to the provisions of the Master Plan.

ARTICLE 3

Plan of Operation

Ninety-two (92) single-family dwelling units were built as shown on the Utopia Plat. Each dwelling unit shares some Common Structural Elements with at least one (1) other unit.

Section 1. Use of Common Area. - - *The* Common Area of Utopia (the "Recreation Area") comprising approximately .4 acres, includes a swimming pool, a bathhouse [with two showers in one stall, separate bathrooms for men and women, a storage room for pool deck furniture in the event of a storm, and an awning attached to one side to shade an otherwise open patio area] and an adjacent deck surrounding the pool. The Common Area also includes: Utopia Drive, the paths to and from the pool area, most of the grounds as well as the archways between units two and three of those four-plex residences with archways and the fences between the walkways leading to units two and three of those four-plex residences with such fences. The archways and fences currently between some units two and three of residential four-plexes are part of the common ground and, as such, the Board's policy shall be to remove rather than repair or replace any of them which are likely to cost more to maintain or repair over a five- year period once damage is detected and to suitably refinish the exterior walls involved. The recreation Area around and including the pool shall be available for use by all Parcel Owners in Utopia, their family members, guests, licensees, and lessees.

Section 2. Rules for the Common Area. - - All common areas and recreational facilities serving any homeowners' association shall be available to parcel owners in the homeowners' association served thereby and their invited guests for the use intended for such common areas and recreational facilities. The entity or entities responsible for the operation of the common areas and recreational facilities may adopt reasonable rules and regulations pertaining to the use of such common areas and recreational facilities. No entity or entities shall unreasonably restrict any parcel owner's right to peaceably assemble or right to invite public officers or candidates for public office to appear and speak in common areas and recreational facilities.

Section 3. Types of Land in Utopia. - - Utopia has two types of land:

- A) Exclusive Common Area owned by the Utopia Property Owners Association, Inc. The Exclusive Common Area includes the described lands, all structures on that land (such as buildings, Utopia Drive, the community pool and pool deck and bathhouse) and all grass, flowers, shrubs and trees on that land, and

- B) Utopia has 92 individually owned Lots with a single-family dwelling on each Lot within a four-plex building. A copy of the original plans is available on microfilm from the Engineering Office of Conch county. The deed for each Lot describes the legal boundaries of that Lot. Those boundaries separate each Lot from both the adjacent privately owned Lot(s) and the commonly owned property. While those legal boundaries officially distinguish private property from common ground, they are not marked on official maps prepared by the various departments of Conch county. A private survey showing the property lines is only required to obtain a mortgage. As those boundaries are complex and vary from one four-plex to another and are only available at considerable expense from private surveyors, the Utopia Property Owners Association, Inc. uses the following guidelines solely for the purpose of directing its agents and employees in carrying out its duty to maintain the Exclusive Common Area.

1) Grounds Maintenance Guideline. - - Grounds maintenance: it is assumed solely for the purposes of grounds maintenance that the boundary between all private property and adjacent Common Ground lies at the foundation of each residence including the patios and carports. The Utopia Property Owners Association, Inc. or its employees, subcontractors or agents will maintain the grounds up to the foundation of each residential building unless the owner(s) alters the garden area(s). Alterations to a garden area are subject to prior written approval of Utopia POAI's Architectural Control Committee. Any owner preferring to maintain their garden area is responsible for notifying the gardeners of that decision and thereafter maintaining their garden area to community standards. Sale of said property causes responsibility to maintain that garden area to revert to the Utopia POA.

2) Garden areas represent a mutual easement between the Utopia Property Owners Association, Inc. and the owners of the private Lots in Utopia. These easements do not in any way advance or justify any claim to either extend the Exclusive Common Area into private property or, conversely, to extend ownership of any private Lot into the original Exclusive Common Area.

3) Tree removal. - - All tree removal must be done by a professionally licensed firm with proper insurance with the written prior approval of the Maintenance Control Committees of both Utopia and IDMA and according to all applicable county and state rules. Homeowners are responsible for the expense of removing any tree s/he either planted or if the shortest and lowest horizontal distance from exterior of the trunk, but not the roots, of any tree s/he did not plant is within three feet of the nearest part the dwelling unit's foundation. Utopia Property Owners Association, Inc. is responsible for removing all other trees at its expense.

Section 4. Operational Priorities. - - the Board of Directors of Utopia's Property Owners Association, Inc. must, as circumstances dictate, shift to one of three different levels of priority within the context of the relevant statutes and its governing documents and the prior decisions of its boards of directors.

- A) Emergencies take precedence or have a preemptive priority over all other Board affairs (that is, routine operations and changes as discussed below) until the emergency is resolved.

    1) Emergencies involving the safety of people in the community or risk of personal injury to residents and their guests have top priority.

    2) Emergencies which only involve damage or risk of damage to common property or infrastructure have second priority and take precedence over emergencies which only involve damage or the risk of damage to residential property in Utopia.

- B) Normal or routine or regularly recurring activities, the usual state of affairs, have secondary priority for the attention of the Board and its committees after emergencies and complete priority over proposals for any sort of change. The Board and its standing committees must deal with such routine matters promptly and aggressively as set forth later in these documents to maintain Utopia in its originally designed and/or later approved altered condition.

- C) Proposals to in any way and to any degree, whether permanently or temporarily, modify, revise, add to or delete, ignore, restate or otherwise alter or change:

    1) the operating procedures or rules of Utopia's Board under these governing documents;

    2) any rules or guidelines or decisions of prior Boards;

    3) any part of the governing documents;

    4) the structure of either the Board in terms of number of Directors and/or officers or the duties of the

Directors and/or officers, or Board committees in terms of the kinds or number of committees, and/or their duties and/or powers, and/or the size of a committee — that is, the number of people serving on that committee;

5) the amount, nature, quality, appearance of common ground including the infrastructure of buildings, roads, sidewalks, paths, irrigation or sprinkler system, sewer system, water system, flower beds, etc.;

6) lead times, content and/or form of notices;

7) eligibility requirements for service on the Board or a Board committee or to vote at a Board or member meeting;

8) voting procedures for Members meetings including those of the Nominating Committee, ways to run for a Directorship, use of an authorized agent, voting and the kinds of ballots that may be used, and counting and monitoring elections; and/or

9) the financial conditions of or relations involving common ground only be addressed after all emergency concerns and routine activities are fully resolved. Even then the Board must act with extreme care and circumspection as specified below.

1) Any proposed change to an item listed immediately above must be fully described in writing in English.

2) Any proposed amendment to an item listed immediately above may only be made by a Member of the community in good standing other than a Director or officer of the Board or Member of a Board committee.

3) That proposal must be presented in writing to the Board or via petition as a call for special meetings of the members to deal only with that proposal. Presentation to the Board at this point is only to assure that all required information is in hand before

transmitting it in a notice for a general or special membership meeting.

4) The proposed change must be fully described and stated in ordinary English or the proposal may not be considered. The purposes, advantages and disadvantages of the proposed change must be clearly stated and each supported by objective and independently verifiable quantitative evidence or the proposal may not be considered.

5) The evidence for the proposed change must objectively show that the proposal would, if implemented, produce a direct net benefit to the majority of the community of at least 30% over and above present practice or the proposal may not be considered. A cost-benefit analysis must be used to establish the net benefit and must ignore any and all purely intangible benefits which cannot be and are not objectively measured by independent and credible experts. Reasonable estimates of foreseeable costs may be used in the analysis. If the costs and/or benefits extend beyond a calendar year, they must be discounted to present value at 6% percent annually after being separately adjusted for their individual risks of occurrence.

6) The proposing party is responsible for obtaining and presenting all of the required evidence at her/his personal expense and bearing the cost of the associated Members' meetings described below. Reimbursement for such costs is only allowable if the proposal is accepted, implemented and yields annual benefits at least as much as claimed for three consecutive years.

7) Any such proposed change must be presented to and approved by two distinct bodies, the Board and the general membership. Two separate special meetings of the Members, one in the daytime and the other in the evening to accommodate working residents, must

be held with proper advance notice including a detailed advance copy of the proposed change to be considered. At least 51% of the members must participate in person or be represented by a duly authorized agent in those membership meetings or those meetings lack a quorum. The proposal fails unless a quorum is established at the scheduled members' meeting(s).

8) The proposed change must be rejected unless both the Board and the general membership meetings independently approve the proposed change.

9) If either the Membership meeting or the Board rejects the proposal, neither it nor any similar proposal may be raised for the next three (3) years.

10) The proposer(s) must be available personally at those Board and Membership meetings to answer questions about the proposed change.

11) Eligible voters or their duly designated agents must vote by secret ballot for or against the proposal at either the general membership meeting or a special membership meeting called solely for that purpose and at which a quorum was established. A supermajority of Members is needed to obtain Membership approval of the proposal or that proposal fails. The requisite supermajority is specified in the amendment section of this document.

12) The proposed change must be addressed in the same fashion at a properly noticed regular or special Board meeting with a quorum established. The Board may only address the proposal if the prior members' meeting approved the proposed change. However, the Board only needs a majority to approve or reject the proposal.

13) The proposed change may not be amended at either the board or general membership meeting(s).

Section 5. Policy Guidelines. - - The Board must consistently operate with a strong bias in favor of the rights of the majority of the community.

A) The Board must actively seek the advice and consent of the Members in formal meetings of the Members and defer to the wishes of the majority or a required supermajority of the Members as expressed in a vote whenever considering a change in the established operating practices of the Board or its committees, any proposed change to the governing documents, or any change to the common area or its use other than routine maintenance and/or repair.

B) No director, or officer of the Board or member of a board committee may accept or rely on personal opinion, judgment, beliefs or preferences in such matters and, if s/he does, has violated her/his fiduciary duty

C) It is a primary responsibility of the President to see that the Directors and Board committee members know their fiduciary responsibilities and honor them or sanction them as specified. This, however, in no way reduces the duties of the other officers and Directors in such matters.

D) Since being a fiduciary generally is an unfamiliar responsibility, any director, officer or committee member will be allowed one (1), but only one (1), breach of their fiduciary duty, whether by omission or commission, during their first term of office before being suspended from Board and/or board committee service pending an appeal. A first apparent violation of a Director's fiduciary duty while in office calls for an immediate warning of possible suspension pending a hearing. A second violation requires suspension pending a hearing which may immediately and permanently declare the offending Director ineligible for all future service on the Board and/or its committees.

1) A suspended director may appeal within 30 business days for a Special Meeting of the Members to be called as soon as possible solely for that purpose or have her/his appeal an agenda item at the next annual meeting of the Members.

2) If the Director appeals, s/he is suspended from all Board service, including voting, until a majority vote of those eligible to vote at the members meeting declares her/him permanently ineligible for Board service or eligible for continued Board service.

3) If a suspended Director fails to appeal within 30 business days of the alleged breach of fiduciary duty, s/he is immediately and permanently ineligible to serve on the Board and/or any of its committees.

E) Tape and/or video recordings of all Board and Members meetings will be made and retained for at least two (2) years in addition to the written Minutes, as evidence of proper or improper behavior. Those recordings are part of the community's public record.

F) If attendance at the meeting(s) where the alleged violation occurred or a review of the recordings of thereof convinces any three (3) former Directors who served at least one full term without ever having been recalled or suspended that a current Director has or persistently violates her/his fiduciary duty without having been suspended by the presiding officer or a majority of the other Directors present, those former Directors may write and sign a petition to the Board which act compels the Board to suspend the suspected violator pending an appeal as described above.

G) If attendance at the meeting(s) where the alleged violation occurred or a review of the recordings of that meeting or meetings convinces at least 33% of the Members that a breach of fiduciary duty occurred, they may sign a petition the Board which compels the Board to suspend the suspected violator pending an appeal as described above.

Section 6. Key Premise and Interpretation. - -

A) The Board must operate on the premise that anything not expressly authorized in these governing documents or attainable by strict conformity to the procedures specified elsewhere to amend these documents is completely forbidden to it. For example, these documents do not expressly allow the Board to start, conduct or fund a publication for the community whether a flyer, newspaper or newsletter. Consequently, the UPOAI cannot do so unless a suitable motion was passed and recorded in the Minutes.

B) If any point in these governing documents yields different interpretations when viewed from a pro-Board perspective versus that of either all or a majority of Members as a group or a minority of Members as a group or even that of an individual Member, the interpretation favoring the interests of:

    1) all Members or a majority thereof shall control or take precedence over all other viewpoints, including a pro-Board one;

    2) a minority of Members shall control or take precedence over the interests of an individual Member as well as that of the Board; and

    3) an individual Member's interests shall control or take precedence over that of the Board.

Section 7. Incorporation of IDMA and Utopia. -- ILLYRIAN DALES MASTER ASSOCIATION, INC. and UTOPIA POA, INC., were incorporated pursuant to Florida Statutes as corporations not for profit. These corporations have the power, among other things, to enforce the Illyrian Dales Declaration and the Utopia Declaration.

ARTICLE 4

Property Rights, Easements and Restrictions

Section 1. Title to Utopia Exclusive Common Area. - - In compliance with Article 3 Section 1 of the Illyrian Dales Declaration, a written commitment which, without limitation,

   A) was executed with the formality of a deed and recorded in the Public Records of Conch county, Florida,

   B) conveyed to the Utopia Exclusive Common Area to Utopia POA, Inc., and

   C) granted to the Owners of Parcels within Utopia the exclusive use and benefit of such Exclusive Common Area.

Section 2. Obligations of members; remedies at law or in equity; levy of fines and suspension of use rights; failure to fill sufficient number of vacancies on board of directors to constitute a quorum; appointment of a receiver on petition of any Member. - -

   A) Each Member and the Member's tenants, guests, and invitees must comply with the Association's governing documents as well as all relevant statutes, ordinances, and case law decisions. Actions at law or in equity, or both, to redress alleged failure or refusal to comply with these provisions may be brought by the Association or by any Member thereof but only after exhausting all other available remedies against:

   1) the Association;

   2) A Member;

   3) Any director or officer of the Association who knowingly or unknowingly fails to comply with these provisions; and

4) Any tenants, guests, or invitees occupying a parcel or using the common areas.

The prevailing party in any such remediation is entitled to recover reasonable attorney's fees and costs. This section does not deprive any person of any other available remedy.

B) The Utopia Property Owners Association, Inc. may suspend for a period of time, not to exceed 90 days per violation, the rights of a Member or a Member's tenants, guests or invitees, or both, to use the common areas and facilities and may levy reasonable fines, not to exceed $100 per initial violation or $1,000 for a repetition of the same violation, against any member or any tenant, guest, or invitees. A separate suspension of common area use rights and/or a fine may be imposed for each incident of continuing violation, with a single notice and opportunity for hearing, except that no such fine shall exceed $1,000 in total for repeating the same violation and no suspension made exceed 90 consecutive calendar days. A fine shall not become a lien against a parcel. In any action to recover a fine, the prevailing party is entitled to collect its reasonable attorney's fees and costs from the nonprevailing party as determined by the court.

1) A fine or suspension of common area use rights may not be imposed without written notice of at least 14 business days to the person sought to be fined or suspended and an opportunity for a hearing before an independent ad hoc committee of at least three members appointed by the board who are not officers, directors, or employees of the association or the spouse, parent, child, or sibling of any serving officer, director or employee. A fine or suspension may only be imposed if approved by a majority vote of the ad hoc review committee.

2) This subsection's requirements do not apply to the imposition of suspensions or fines on any Member for failure of that Member to pay assessments or other charges when due.

3) Suspension of common-area use rights shall not impair the right of a Member or tenant of a parcel to have vehicular and pedestrian ingress to and egress from the parcel, including, but not limited to, the right to park.

C) Utopia may suspend a member's voting rights for nonpayment of regular and/or special assessments that are delinquent for more than 90 calendar days.

Section 3. Easements of Enjoyment. - - Every Utopia Lot Owner has an easement of enjoyment in and to Utopia's Exclusive Common Area which right is related to and shall pass with the title to such Parcel, subject to the following:

A) The right of Utopia POA, Inc. (in accordance with its Declaration of Maintenance Covenants, Articles of Incorporation and Bylaws), to borrow money for the purpose of improving the Exclusive Common Area which it owns, and in aid thereof, to mortgage such property;

B) The right of Utopia POA, Inc. to take such steps as are reasonably necessary to protect the Exclusive Common Area against foreclosures;

C) The right of Utopia POA, Inc. to dedicate or transfer title to all or any part of the Exclusive Common Area which it owns to any public agency, authority, or utility;

D) All provisions of this Utopia Declaration, the Articles of Incorporation and Bylaws of Utopia POA, Inc.;

E) Rules and regulations governing the use and enjoyment of the Exclusive Common Area as may be adopted by Utopia POA, Inc. from time to time;

F) Restrictions, easements and other matters contained on any and all plats of the lands constituting Illyrian Dales; and

G) The right of Utopia POA, Inc. to suspend an Owner's voting rights and his right to use the Exclusive Common Area for any period during which an assessment against his Lot remains unpaid, and for a period not to exceed ninety (90) days for any single or initial infraction of its published rules and regulations.

Section 4. Easements for Building Encroachments and Common Structural Elements. -- Each Lot and the Exclusive Common Area shall be subject to an easement for encroachments created by construction, settling and overhangs for all buildings in Utopia. A valid easement for such encroachments and for their maintenance shall exist for so long as the encroachments exist. In the event that a building is partially or totally destroyed and then rebuilt, the Owners of dwelling units in the building so affected agree that minor encroachments of parts of the adjacent dwelling units or Exclusive Common Area due to construction shall be permitted, and that a valid easement for such encroachment and the maintenance thereof shall exist.

Each Lot and the Common Area at Utopia shall be subject to an easement of support and use over, upon, across, under, through and into the Common Structural Elements in favor of Utopia POA, Inc., the dwelling unit Owners and their employees, servants, agents and designees for the continued use, benefit, enjoyment, support, service, maintenance, repair and design of all dwelling units and the Common Structural Elements in Utopia. Such easements include the right of a suitably licensed and insured firm or board representative or employee to enter a residence or stand on its roof during reasonable hours and with reasonable advance notice to effect necessary maintenance or repairs on a common wall or adjacent roof or perform health or safety inspections as well as but not limited to preventing rodent or insect infestations.

Section 5. Reservation of Right to Grant Easements and Licenses. - - Utopia Property Owners Association, Inc. hereby reserves unto itself and its assignees the right to grant easements, both temporary and permanent, over the Exclusive Common Area in favor of itself, public and quasi-public authorities, utility companies and franchisees, as well as the right to grant licenses and rights-of-way to the foregoing persons and entities as well as their family members, guests, licensees, invitees, lessees, servants, agents and employees.

Utopia Property Owners Association, Inc. [UPOAI] or its assignees have the right to grant such casements and/or licenses as it deems reasonably necessary or appropriate to carry out the provisions of the Master Plan and its responsibilities under these governing documents. None of the grantees of an easement or license named in this Section have the right to assign its easement or license, or any benefits thereof, without the prior written approval of UPOAI.

Section 6. Restrictions on Dwelling Unit Leases. - - Any and all lease agreements ("lease") between an Owner and a Lessee of the Owner's dwelling unit at Utopia shall be in writing and must provide that it shall be subject in all respects to the terms and provisions of the Utopia Documents and that any failure by the lessee to comply with their terms and provisions shall be a material default and breach of the lease. An owner may only lease his Utopia residence:

- A) if not in arrears on dues, maintenance fees, special assessments, or fines;

- B) once in any 12 consecutive months starting with the inception the first lease s/he issues;

- C) for a term of at least ninety (90) consecutive days but not more than one year with at most one option to renew for the same interval;

D) if and only if the lease provides that the lessee thereunder pay any and all Association Expenses and/or assessments levied against the dwelling unit at Utopia directly to UPOAI; and

E) if and only if the Utopia Property Owners Association, Inc., in its sole judgment, approves the prospective tenant's suitability from data in the public domain and/or a standard form submitted by the prospective tenant.

F) Notwithstanding the obligation of the lessee to make such payments directly to the Property Owners Association, the owner remains primarily liable for the payment of any and all such Association Expenses and/or assessments until they are paid.

Section 7. Restrictions on Dwelling Unit Sales. - -

A) Each and every time an Owner intends to make a sale of his dwelling unit at Utopia or any interest therein, he ("Offeror") shall give written notice to Utopia POA, Inc. of such intention ("Notice"), together with the name and address of the intended purchaser, the terms of such purchase and such other information as the Property Owners Association may reasonably require on forms supplied by it ("Offering"). The giving of such Notice shall constitute a warranty and representation by the Offeror to Utopia POA, Inc. as hereinafter provided, that the Offering is a bona fide sale in all respects. The Notice shall be given by certified mail, return receipt requested, or delivered by hand to the Secretary of Utopia POA, Inc., who shall give a receipt therefor.

B) Utopia Property Owners Association, Inc. must screen and interview prospective buyers as to their suitability to buy a residence in the community according to established standards and obtain written confirmation of the potential buyer's willingness to obey the rules set forth in the governing documents prior to any sale. The UPOAI may in its sole judgment approve or disapprove a prospective buyer. The cost of such screening is limited to the application fee.

C) Within thirty (30) days after receipt of the Notice, the Utopia Board, will either approve the Offering ("Approval") or furnish to the Offeror by written notice (the "Substitution Notice") the name and address of a purchaser approved by it to accept the terms of the Offering ("Substituted Purchaser").

    1) The Approval ("Certificate of Approval") must be written in recordable form signed by any two (2) members of the Utopia Board and be delivered to the Offeror and the proposed Purchaser named in the Offering. Failure of the Utopia Board to grant Approval or to furnish a Substituted Purchaser within thirty business (30) days after the Notice is given shall constitute Approval of the Offering, and the Property Owners Association shall be required to prepare and deliver the Certificate of Approval to the Offeror and the purchaser of the Offeror named in the Offering.

    2) If UPOAI furnishes the Offeror the Substitution Notice, the Offeror will be deemed to have made the Offering to the Substituted Purchaser; provided however, that the Substituted Purchaser has at least thirty (30) business days after the date of the Substitution Notice to consummate the sale of the Offeror's dwelling unit in Utopia. The Offeror shall be obligated to consummate the Offering with the Substituted Purchaser on terms no less favorable than the terms stated in the Offering, and the Offeror shall not be relieved of such obligation except upon the written consent of the Property Owners Association and the Substituted Purchaser. Upon closing with the Substituted Purchaser, Utopia POA, Inc. shall deliver its Certificate of Approval.

    3) In the event the Substituted Purchaser furnished by the Property Owners Association shall default in his obligation to purchase such dwelling unit at Utopia, Utopia POA, Inc. shall prepare and deliver the Certificate of Approval to the Offeror and the purchaser of the Offeror named in the Offering.

Section 8. Enforceability of Certain Covenants. -- Except for the enforcement of the lien for assessments, the covenants in this Utopia Declaration may be enforced by the Utopia POA, Inc. or, in the event UPOAI declines to enforce these covenants within 30 calendar days of the offense, following a written request to enforce, signed by not less than twenty-five percent (25%) of the Owners of dwelling units in Utopia, then the Owners who signed that petition are free to attempt to collectively enforce compliance with such covenants in the appropriate court of law or by means of any other dispute reconciliation measures available to them.

Section 9. General Federal Home Loan Mortgage Corporation {FHLMC} Requirements. --

> A) The Federal Home Loan Mortgage Corporation prohibits The Utopia Property Owners Association, Inc. [UPOAI] from exercising certain powers, by act or omission, over the Common Area unless and until all of the requirements below are fully satisfied. Those requirements must be completely satisfied before considering, let alone implementing any proposal to alter or improve — but not maintain or repair — the Common Area, including any structures such as the bathhouse, road, irrigation/sprinkler system and so forth, as to amount of property owned, qualities or characteristics of some or all of that property, use(s) of some or all of that property, and/or any financial arrangements relying on some or all of that property including collateralization of some or all of that property. To satisfy the FHLMC's requirements, the UPOAI must see that all of the following conditions are fulfilled exactly as specified and in the order shown.
>
>> 1) A complete description of the proposed alteration and its purpose(s) written in ordinary English must be provided to the Board by the individual(s) advocating that change. Said description must be prepared at the proposer's expense and must be available to all members of the community.
>>
>> 2) The Board may only authorize reimbursement of the expenses of preparing the description of the proposed

alteration if the project is approved as described below and successfully completed.

3) The proposer may not be a current Director or officer of the Board or the chairman or a member of any standing committee of the Board.

4) The description of the project must include:

> [a] all architectural blueprints, renderings, lists and other materials needed to obtain the necessary permits and to guide suitably licensed and insured contractors in their bidding and doing the work;
>
> [b] a diagram of the project's critical path from start to completion;
>
> [c] a budget based on firm written bids from at least three qualified contractors for each part of the project;
>
> [d] a narrative rationale for the project which objectively establishes that the community will gain a net benefit at least 30% greater by doing the project than not doing it based on a standard economic cost-benefit analysis which only includes for consideration the asserted benefits that are objective measured or valued and verifiably correct according to independent experts; and
>
> [e] a Lorenz-Gini Coefficient from modern economics of no more than 0.2000 to show that the asserted objective benefits will be spread reasonably equitably across the owners.

These documents must be in hand and available for homeowner's inspection at the Association Office at least 30 business days before any such proposed alteration may move to the second step in its evaluation.

B) The second step in evaluating any such project is a formal review and approval or rejection by the Architectural and/or Maintenance Control Committees of the Board, if appropriate. Those committees must review the proposal in duly noticed open meetings and decide by formal majority vote whether or not to approve the proposal for review by the Board prior to transmission to and consideration by the membership at a general or special meeting of the membership.

> 1) If rejected by the appropriate committee(s), the original proposal may be revised once and once only and resubmitted once and once only for reconsideration within 30 business days.
>
> 2) In any event, the decision(s) of the committee(s) must be supported by a logical and factually based written explanation submitted to the Board with 30 business days of the committee's review of the proposal to be valid. The Board must accept and respect that decision.
>
> 3) Assuming approval by the appropriate committee(s) or the clear lack of need to involve those committees, the Board must schedule a meeting of the membership to review and discuss the project and vote to approve or disapprove the project.
>
>> [a] Notice of the Members meeting must include copies of all relevant documents and be sent at least 30 business days before the scheduled annual or special members meeting.
>>
>> [b] Members may attend and vote in person or be represented by a duly authorized agent who is to be counted toward the establishment of a quorum, allowed to speak for their principal, and allowed to cast a ballot for their principal.
>>
>> [c] At least two-thirds of the owners eligible to vote must approve the project for it to move ahead; otherwise the project fails.

4) If the membership meeting approves the proposal, the Board must next conduct a census at the proposer's expense of the members to ascertain which homeowners have a mortgage and the contact information for those mortgagees.

5) The Board must then write those mortgagees to inform them of the proposed alteration and solicit their approval in writing or at a special meeting of their representatives. The proposed change fails unless the mortgagees approve the proposed project by at least a two-thirds majority independently of and subsequent to a favorable vote by the membership.

6) If and only if the proposed project has survived to this point, the Board must review the proposal and vote to approve or disapprove it based on the ability to fund the project without imposing an undue burden on the community's finances.

7) If and only if the proposed project obtains approval of the appropriate committee(s), Membership, and Board in that order, the Board must submit the proposal to IDMA's Architectural Control Committee with written certification signed by the President of the Board that the proposal has passed all of the above requirements.

8) If and only if the proposed project is approved by IDMA's Architectural Control Committee's approval, may the Board meet to consider adopting the proposal by majority vote, assign responsibility for supervising the project, authorize application(s) for all necessary permits, and arrange funding.

B) Unless and until all of the above requirements are met exactly as specified, the Utopia POA, Inc. shall not be entitled to:

1) By act or omission seek to abandon, partition, subdivide, encumber, sell or transfer any portion of

the Common Area within Utopia owned, directly or indirectly by Utopia POA, Inc. (the granting of easements for public utilities or for other Public purposes consistent with the intended use of such Common Area shall not be deemed to be a transfer within the meaning of this clause);

2) Change the method of determining the obligations, assessments, dues or other charges which may be levied against a Lot at Utopia or its Owner;

3) By act or omission change, waive or abandon any scheme of regulation or enforcement thereof, pertaining to the architectural design or the exterior appearance of units, the exterior maintenance of units, the maintenance of the common property, party walks or common fences and driveways or the upkeep of lawns and plantings at Utopia;

4) Fail to maintain fire and extended coverage on insurable Common Area Property at Utopia on a current replacement cost basis in an amount not less than one hundred percent (100%) of the insurable value (based on current replacement cost); or

5) Use hazard insurance proceeds for losses to any Common Area property at Utopia for other than the repair, replacement or reconstruction of such common Property.

6) Any "right of first refusal" including without limitation the restrictions contained in Article 4's Sections 6 and 7, shall not impair the rights of a first mortgagee of an improved or unimproved lot or parcel in Utopia to foreclose or take title to such Mortgaged Lot pursuant to the remedies provided in its mortgage, or accept a deed (or assignment) in lieu of foreclosure in the event of default by a mortgagor or sell or lease a Mortgaged Lot acquired by such mortgagee.

7) Any first mortgagee who obtains title to a Mortgaged Lot pursuant to the remedies provided in its mortgage

or a foreclosure of the mortgage will not be liable for such Mortgaged Lot's unpaid dues, charges or assessments which accrued prior to the acquisition of title to such Mortgaged Lot by the mortgagee.

8) No unit owner, or any party, shall have priority over any rights of the first mortgagee of a unit, in the case of a distribution to such unit owner of insurance proceeds or condemnation awards for losses to or a taking of common property.

9) All Property Owners Association dues, assessments or charges shall include an adequate reserve fund for maintenance, repairs and replacement of those elements of the Exclusive Common Area that must be replaced on a periodic basis. Such dues, assessments or charges shall be payable in regular installments or, at the owner's option, by a single payment. Such funds shall not be commingled or used for other than their originally designated purpose.

10) Utopia POA, Inc., upon request, shall furnish written notification to a first institutional mortgagee of any default in the performance by a Lot Owner-Borrower of any obligation under the Utopia Documents which is not cured within sixty calendar days.

Section 10. FHLMC Insurance Requirements. - -

A) The Property Owners Association must have fire and extended coverage insurance for no less than 100% of replacement cost of insurable Exclusive Common Area property. Such insurance must name as the insured, Utopia POA, Inc. for the benefit of the dwelling unit owners.

B) The Property Owners Association must have fidelity coverage against dishonest acts on the part of directors, managers, trustees, employees or volunteers responsible for handling funds collected and held for the benefit of the dwelling unit owners. The fidelity bond or insurance must name the Property Owners Association as the named insured and shall be written in an amount sufficient to provide protection which is in no event less than one and one-half times the insured estimated annual operating expenses and reserves. In connection with such coverage, an appropriate endorsement to the policy to cover any persons who serve without compensation shall be added if the policy would not otherwise cover volunteers.

C) The Property Owners Association must have a comprehensive policy of public liability insurance covering all of the Exclusive Common Area property. Such insurance shall contain a "severability of interest" clause or endorsement which shall preclude the insurer from denying the claim of a dwelling unit owner because of negligent acts of the Property Owners Association, or other dwelling unit owners. The scope of coverage must include all other coverage in the kind and amounts commonly required by private institutional mortgage investors for Planned Unit Developments similar in construction, location and use. Coverage shall be for at least $1,000,000.00 per occurrence for personal injury and/or property damage.

D) Every three (3) years or less from the date of recording this document, The Board of Directors of UPOAI must review its liability, property and fidelity insurance to determine if it has adequate coverage and correct any insufficiency found.

Section 11. Other FHLMC Requirements. - -

A) Any agreement for professional community management of Utopia or any other contract, may not exceed three years. Further, any such agreement must provide for termination by either party without cause and without payment of a termination fee on thirty days or less written notice.

B) If requested, the Property Owners Association will provide to an institutional first mortgagee a list containing the name and permanent residence address of each individual or entity which owns or is under contract to purchase a dwelling unit at Utopia.

Section 12. Prospective purchasers subject to association membership requirement, disclosure required, covenants, assessments, contract cancellation. - -

- A) A prospective purchaser of property in Utopia must be presented a disclosure summary and copy of the governing documents before executing the contract for sale and must acknowledge in writing at the time of the sale not only receipt of that document but that s/he/they have read and understood it and agree to obey and enforce its rules. The general form of the disclosure summary is available in the 2004 Florida Statute 720.401. The receipt is to be delivered to the UPOAI for its records. The seller must provide a copy of the disclosure summary and governing documents at their expense and at least 30 calendar days prior to consummation of the sale.

ARTICLE 5

Requirements for Contracts

Section 1. Relevant Contracts. - - All contracts as further described in this section or any contract that is not to be fully performed within one (1) calendar year after the making thereof for the purchase, lease, or renting of materials or equipment to be used by the Association in accomplishing its purposes under these governing documents, and all contracts for the provision of services, must be written in plain English.

- A) The Association must obtain three (3) competitive bids for the equipment, materials and/or services of any such contract which requires payment by the Association that in total exceeds 10 percent of the total annual budget of the association, including reserves.

- B) Nothing in this section shall be construed to require the Association to accept the lowest bid. However, in the event that the Association accepts a bid higher than the lowest one, the Association must state for the record all of its reasons for accepting that bid and rejecting the lowest one.

Section 2. Exceptions. - -

A) Contracts with employees of the association, and contracts for attorney, accountant, architect, community association manager, engineering, and landscape architect services are exempt from the provisions of Section 1 immediately above.

B) A contract executed before October 1, 2004, and any renewal thereof is exempt from the competitive bid requirements of Section 1 of this article. If a contract was awarded under the competitive bid procedures of this article, any renewal of that contract is exempt from such competitive bid requirements if the contract contains a provision that allows the board to cancel the contract on 30 days' notice. Materials, equipment, or services provided to an association under a local government franchise agreement by a franchise holder are exempt from the competitive bid requirements of this article. A contract with a manager, if made by competitive bid, may be made for no longer than three (3) years and may not contain a provision for automatic renewal. An association whose declaration or bylaws provide for competitive bidding for services may operate under those provisions in lieu of this article if those provisions are at least as stringent as the requirements of this article.

C) Nothing contained in this article is intended to limit UPAOI from obtaining needed products and/or services in an emergency.

D) This article does not apply if the business entity with which UPOAI desires to enter into a contract is the only source of supply within Conch County.

E) Nothing in this article excuses a party contracting to provide maintenance or community management services from compliance with Florida statute 720.309.

Section 3. Contracts with Community Management firms. - - All relationships with any community management service must be memorialized in a written contract. That contract may not automatically renew. Any such contract and changes proposed to it must be completely reviewed during a Board meeting to be held at least every two years. No such contract can include requiring or relying on or deferring to or paying for advice, consulting or guidance as to the application, meaning, interpretation, consequences or implications of any relevant law(s) or the governing documents by the Community Management Service.

Section 4. Contractor Standards. - - Only properly licensed and insured firms with at least five years of experience may do any work for the Board, its committees or any resident. The credentials of such firms must be established with and approved in writing by the Board or its appropriate committee(s) as well as IDMA's Architectural Control Committee before any contracts are made, permits obtained and posted, or work started.

ARTICLE 6

Utopia Property Owners Association

Section 1. Not-for-profit corporation. - - ILLYRIAN DALES MASTER ASSOCIATION, INC. [IDMA], a not-for-profit corporation incorporated in Utopia, has by virtue of its Articles and Bylaws authority to provide for the exercise of architectural control of improvements constructed in Illyrian Dales. The functions, duties, responsibilities, and powers of the Association, as to Utopia, are hereby delegated by the Association to, and assumed by, Utopia POA, Inc. but the proper performance of such functions, duties, responsibilities and powers are a continuing condition and requirement for the efficacy of such delegation and assumption.

Section 2. Intervention by IDMA. - - If Illyrian Dales Master Association, Inc. determines, in its sole discretion, that Utopia POA, Inc. is not properly performing any of its functions, duties, responsibilities or powers, the Association may revoke wholly or in part any of such functions, duties, responsibilities or powers and exercise control over the improvements constructed in Utopia. Without restricting the foregoing, the Association shall have the authority and right to enforce any provision or covenant in this

Declaration, including those relating to assessments and the foreclosure of liens.

[As a practical matter, IDMA limits its exercise of the powers reserved to it above to two situations. The primary application of those powers involves settling disputes between two or more subdivisions of Illyrian Dales which operate under disparate governing documents. The secondary application of those powers concerns review and approval of proposed architectural changes by IDMA's Architectural Control Committee [ACC]. In such cases, IDMA's ACC acts to assure the following requirements.

> First, that the change(s) sought satisfy the established architectural standards of both the subdivision and IDMA.
> Second, the contractor(s) meets established licensing and insurance standards.
> Third, the proposed alterations are structurally sound.

IDMA's ACC has to assume that proposals sent for its review were prepared according to due process and accepted by Utopia's homeowners in accordance with established due process.

These policies arise from IDMA's financial and technical limitations as well as the impracticality of it displacing all of the various governance arrangements already in place at the various Illyrian Dales subdivisions and trying to equitably govern each and every subdivision according to its unique situation and governing documents.]

Section 3. Directors Are Fiduciaries of Members. - - The officers, directors and committee members of UPOAI have a fiduciary relationship to the Members who are served by the Association. The powers and duties of UPOAI include those set forth in this declaration and other governing documents except as limited or restricted by local, county, state and/or federal law.

Section 4. Legal Actions. - -

A) UPOAI may institute, maintain, settle, or appeal actions or hearings in its name on behalf of all Members concerning matters of common interest to the members, including, but not limited to the common areas; roof or structural components of a commonly owned building, or other modifications for which the association is responsible; mechanical, electrical, or plumbing elements serving a modification or building for which the Association is responsible; and protesting ad valorem taxes on commonly used facilities.

B) UPOAI may defend actions in eminent domain or bring inverse condemnation actions.

C) The Association must first obtain the affirmative approval of a majority of the voting interests at a properly noticed meeting of the membership at which a quorum has been attained before commencing litigation against any party in the name of the association which may in total involve amounts, including potential legal fees and costs for all parties in excess of $10,000.

D) This section does not limit any statutory or common-law right of any individual Member or class of Members to bring an action without participation by the association. A Member does not have the right to act for UPOAI by virtue of being a Member.

ARTICLE 7

Maintenance and Repair Obligations

Section 1. General. - - In addition to its future responsibilities as owner of the Utopia Exclusive Common Area, Utopia POA, Inc. is responsible for and obligated to maintain, repair and replace:

A) the exterior finish on the surfaces of Multiplex buildings;

B) the lawns, driveways and sprinkler systems in and on the

Utopia Lots; and

C) the landscaping of all Lots according to an updated and current landscaping plan of Utopia, but excluding therefrom any landscaping not provided for in Utopia's Master Landscape Plan or which lies on private property and has been suitably marked by the Owner to show that s/he will have it cared for by another at the Owner's expense.

1) Any landscaping plan is suspended until hurricane damage and tree removal and replacement is effected to the satisfaction of the grounds maintenance committee, the arborist doing the work and the county. A new landscaping plan must be created within 90 business days after this disruption was corrected and submitted for county review and approval. That new landscaping plan supplants and replaces all prior landscaping plans once it is approved by the county.

2) Replacement of foliage and trees will be at the sole discretion of UPOAI and its grounds maintenance committee provided such replacement(s) conform to the recommendations of the arborist and county rules and regulations.

Section 2. Damage Caused by an Owner, Tenant, Guest, etc. - - In the event Utopia POA, Inc. determines that the need for maintenance, repair or replacement of any of the items described in this Article has been caused through the willful or negligent act of the Owner, his family, or their employees, agents, servants, guests, invitees or lessees, the cost of such maintenance, repair or replacement shall become a part of the assessment to be levied against such Owner's Lot and shall not be the joint responsibility of all Utopia Owners.

ARTICLE 8

Covenants for Assessments

Section 1. Creation of the Lien and Personal Obligation for the Assessments. - - Utopia POA, Inc. shall have the power to collect assessments which it levies

    A) against all Utopia dwelling units and their Owners, and which are therefore shared on a pro rata basis, and

    B) against an individual Utopia dwelling unit and its Owners. Each Owner of a Utopia dwelling unit and Lot hereby covenant and agree to the following provisions:

        1) Each shall pay all assessments levied against any Utopia Parcel which it owns.

        2) There shall be an annual assessment established by the Utopia Board, as well as special assessments as deemed by the Utopia Board to be instrumental to carrying out its responsibilities pursuant to this Declaration.

        3) Utopia POA, Inc. shall have a lien for all such assessments, together with interest thereon from the due date at the simple annual rate of ten percent (10%), and the costs of collection thereof including costs and reasonable attorneys' fees at trial and appellate levels, upon the Parcels against which each such assessment is made.

        4) No Owner may avoid or otherwise escape liability for the assessments provided for herein by his nonuse or abandonment of the Exclusive Common Area.

Section 2. Purpose of Assessments. - - The assessments levied and to be collected by Utopia POA, Inc. shall be used for the purpose of promoting the recreation, health, safety and welfare of the Utopia Lot Owners, for providing exterior maintenance to wall surfaces but not the roofs of Utopia dwelling units and for maintenance of the Exclusive Common Area, including but not limited to, the cost of taxes, insurance, security, labor, equipment, materials, management, maintenance, repair, replacement and supervision thereof, as well as for such other purposes as are permissible activities of Utopia POA, Inc. and undertaken by it.

Section 3. CAP on Improvements. - - Notwithstanding any other provisions of this Article 8, the Utopia Board is only authorized to expend Association funds for special improvement projects and/or capital improvements, so long as appropriate due process as described elsewhere was followed exactly and the yearly total expenditure for the projects do not exceed the CAP (as hereinafter described) unless an appropriate affirmative vote of the members was obtained. The CAP during the first year after the effective date of amendment shall be $1,000. The CAP in each year thereafter shall be $1,000 plus/minus an increase/decrease based on the Consumer Price Index for the Miami-Fort Lauderdale consolidated metropolitan statistical area from the effective date to the beginning of a subsequent year. (Multiply the base figure of $1,000 by the year-to-year percentage change in the above consumer price index to obtain the new figure.) The U.S. Department of Labor's Bureau of Labor Statistics is the official source of this data series.

Expenditures for special improvement projects and capital improvements collectively totaling in excess of the CAP shall not be made without following exactly and successfully the evaluation process for such projects described elsewhere, including an affirmative vote of a supermajority as described elsewhere of the entire voting membership of the Association at a special meeting of the members duly called solely for such purpose. No special meeting of the members may be called for this purpose until all members have received and had at least 30 business days to review and consider a fully detailed description of the proposed project and written assurance signed by the President of the Board that the specified review process to date was followed exactly. The due date, manner and method of payment of such excess expenditure shall be fixed by the voting membership when approval is required in excess of the CAP.

Section 4. CAP on Attorney's Fees. - - Notwithstanding any other provisions of this Article 8, the Utopia Board is only authorized to expend Association funds for attorney's fees and/or services, so long as appropriate due process as described elsewhere was followed exactly and the yearly total expenditure for the projects do not exceed the CAP (as hereinafter described) unless an appropriate affirmative vote of the Members was obtained. The CAP during the first year after the effective date of amendment shall be $4,140 [92 households * $45.00/household/year] with certain exceptions. Legal expenses incurred by the Association to defend itself against actions brought by individuals who are neither homeowners nor residents are exempt from the CAP save for actions brought by an Ombudsman, if there is one. Legal expenses incurred to review, update and record revised governing documents are exempt from the CAP once every decade from the time of recording these governing documents. Legal expenses to deal with tax matters and/or emergencies are exempt from the CAP. The CAP applies to legal fees for attorney's advice and/or actions against homeowners or residents. The CAP in each year thereafter shall be $4,140 plus/minus an increase/decrease based on the Consumer Price Index for the Miami-Fort Lauderdale consolidated metropolitan statistical area from the effective date to the beginning of a subsequent year. (Multiply the base figure of $4,140 by the year-to-year percentage change in the above consumer price index to obtain the new figure.) The U.S. Department of Labor's Bureau of Labor Statistics is the official source of this data series.

Annual expenditures for attorney's fees and/services collectively totaling in excess of the CAP shall not be made without following exactly and successfully the evaluation process for such projects described elsewhere including an affirmative vote of a supermajority as described elsewhere of the entire voting membership of the Association at a special meeting of the Members duly called solely for such purpose. No special meeting of the members may be called for this purpose until all Members have received and had at least 30 business days to review and consider a fully detailed description of the proposed legal action and written assurance signed by the President of the Board that the specified review process to date was followed exactly. The due date, manner and method of payment of such excess expenditure shall be fixed by the voting membership when approval is required in excess of the CAP.

Section 5. Annual Assessments. - - The annual assessment, which may include funds for special improvement projects and for capital improvements, shall be proposed on a yearly basis by the Utopia Board and approved by an appropriate affirmative vote of the membership at a meeting which had suitable advance notice and at which a quorum existed at the time of the vote and shall commence on the date (which shall be the first day of a month) fixed by the Utopia Board to be the date of commencement.

The annual assessments shall be payable in advance, but may be paid in periodic installments if so determined by the Utopia Board.

Section 6. Special Assessments. - - Only one special assessment in furtherance of this Association's purposes may be levied in any fiscal year by the Utopia Board and then only to finance emergency maintenance and/or repairs to the common ground; any special assessment to obtain reimbursement from a Lot Owner for damage s/he or her/his guests, invitees or employees caused to the common ground is exempt from this restriction, that is, as many such individualized special assessments may be imposed in any given year as are found necessary. The due date, manner and method of payment of any special assessment shall be fixed in the resolution authorizing the assessment. A special assessment may be levied pro rata against all Lot Owners or it may be levied against one or more Lot Owners pursuant to Article 7 Maintenance and Repair. Under no circumstances may part of all of any special assessment be used to fund all or part of a special improvement, capital improvement or any reserve fund.

Section 7. Apportionment of Assessments. - - The annual assessments and the special assessments provided for herein shall be apportioned on a pro rata basis on all Utopia Lots as of the date the Utopia Board creates the assessment.

The parties recognize that certain Lots located at Utopia will have a greater amount of square footage than others and that certain dwelling units will be larger than others and vary in amenities. However, the parties agree that each lot shall be assessed on an equal basis with all other Lots in Utopia, regardless of any differences. This provision shall not apply to assessments levied pursuant to section 2 of Article 7, Maintenance and Repair Obligations.

Section 8. Status of Assessments. - - Utopia POA, Inc. shall furnish to any Owner upon his demand a certificate in writing signed by one of its officers setting forth the status of assessments against that Owner's Parcel. This certificate shall be conclusive evidence of payment of any assessment therein stated to have been paid. No charge shall be imposed for such certificates.

Section 9. Effect of and Remedies for Nonpayment of Assessments. - - If an assessment is not paid on the date when due, such assessment shall then become delinquent and shall, together with interest thereon and costs of collection thereof, become a continuing lien on the Parcel as set forth in this Article.

A) If the assessment is not paid within thirty business (30) days after the due date, Utopia POA, Inc. may bring an action to establish and record the lien against the Parcel in the proper court. There shall be added to the amount of such assessment the costs of preparing and filing the complaint in such action.

B) A lien may only be foreclosed if it exceeds 20% of the current price of the residence in question, said current price based on the average of three independent appraisers, without taking fines, legal fees and costs into account. In the event a judgment is obtained, such judgment shall include interest at the simple annual rate of ten percent (10%) on the assessment as provided for in this Article, and a reasonable attorney's fee (including fees for appeals) to be fixed by the court together with the costs of the action.

C) Nothing contained herein shall prevent Utopia POA, Inc. from simultaneously exercising any other election or pursuing any other remedy which it may have to accomplish the same end.

Section 10. Subordination of the Lien to Mortgages. - - The lien of the assessments provided for herein shall be subordinate to the lien of any bona fide first mortgage or mortgages (except from buyer to seller of a Parcel) but superior to any second mortgage or mortgages now or hereafter placed upon the Parcel subject to assessment; provided, however, that such subordination shall apply only to the assessments which have become due and payable prior to a sale or transfer of such Parcel pursuant to a judgment of foreclosure or prior to a deed given in lieu of foreclosure. No sale or transfer shall relieve any Parcel from liability for any assessments thereafter becoming due, nor from the lien of any such subsequent assessment.

Any first mortgagee may, singly or with other first mortgagees, pay any taxes, assessments or other charges which are in default and which may or have become due against the Exclusive Common Area, and it may pay overdue premiums on hazard insurance policies or secure new hazard insurance coverage on the lapse of a policy thereon. In such event, the first mortgagee making such payments shall be owed immediate reimbursement therefor from Utopia POA, Inc.

Section 11. Exempt Property. - - The following property subject to this Declaration shall be exempted from all assessments and liens created herein:

- A) any easement or other interest therein dedicated and accepted by the local public authority and devoted to public use;

- B) all Exclusive Common Area as defined in Article 1 hereof; and

- C) all properties exempted from ad valorem taxation by the laws of the State of Florida, to the extent agreed to by Utopia POA, Inc.

Section 12. Termination of Assessment Liens. - - If not sooner terminated by action of law or by release or payment, any lien for an assessment made pursuant to the provisions of this Utopia Declaration shall terminate ten (10) years after the date of such assessment unless an action for the enforcement thereof shall have been brought prior to the expiration of such ten (10) year period.

Section 13. Two-year Assessments and Capped as to Increases. - - Starting in the second year after recording these governing documents, maintenance assessments must be established for two-year periods, barring an emergency, and may not be raised in any given fiscal year by more than $50 per household per month above the local rate of inflation compared to the prior fiscal year. The rate of inflation to be used is the Consumer Price Index for the Miami-Fort Lauderdale consolidated metropolitan statistical area supplied by the U.S. Department of Labor's Bureau of Labor Statistics which is the official source of this data series.

ARTICLE 9

General Provisions

Section 1. Duration. - - The covenants and conditions of this Declaration shall run with and bind the land herein defined as Utopia and inure to the benefit of Utopia POA, Inc., the Owners, mortgagees and their respective legal representatives, heirs, successors and assigns for a term expiring on March 29, 2051 after which time this Declaration shall be automatically renewed and extended for successive periods of ten (10) years each, unless at least one (1) year prior to the termination of the term or any such ten (10) year extension thereof there is recorded amongst the Public Records of Conch county, Florida, an instrument (the "Termination Instrument") signed by at least two-thirds (2/3) of all Owners and at least two-thirds (2/3) of all mortgagees holding mortgages encumbering Parcels (on the basis of one vote for each mortgage) agreeing to terminate this Declaration, upon which event, this Declaration shall be terminated upon the expiration of the original term or the ten (10) year extension thereof during which the Termination Instrument is recorded.

Section 2. Notices. - - Any notice required to be sent to any Member or Owner under the provisions of this Utopia Declaration will be deemed to have been properly sent when mailed, postpaid, to the last known address of the person or entity who appears as a Member or Owner on the records of Utopia POA, Inc. at the time of such mailing. A copy of such notice will also be sent to Utopia POA, Inc. and Illyrian Dales Master Association, Inc.

Section 3. Dispute Resolution. - -

    A) All alternative means of dispute resolution available must be tried and exhausted before bringing suit in a court. Filing a petition for mediation or arbitration will toll the applicable statute of limitations.

        1) Any recall dispute filed with the department pursuant to Florida Statute 720.303 (10) will be conducted by the department in accordance with the provisions of Florida Statutes 718.112 (2)(j) and 718.1255 and the rules adopted by the division.

        2) In addition, the department will conduct mandatory binding arbitration of election disputes between a Member and the UPOAI pursuant to Florida Statute 718.1255 and rules adopted by the division.

        3) Neither election disputes nor recall disputes are eligible for mediation: these disputes will be arbitrated by the department. At the conclusion of the proceeding, the department will charge the parties a fee in an amount adequate to cover all costs and expenses incurred by the department in conducting the proceeding. Initially the petitioner will remit a filing fee of at least $200 to the department. The fees paid to the department will become a non recoverable cost in the arbitration proceeding, and the prevailing party in an arbitration proceeding will recover its reasonable costs and attorney's fees in an amount found reasonable by the arbitrator. The department will adopt rules to effectuate the purposes of this section.

B) Disputes between an association and a parcel owner regarding use of or changes to the parcel of common areas and other covenant enforcement disputes, disputes regarding amendments to the association's governing documents, disputes regarding meetings of the board and committees appointed by the board, membership meetings not including election meetings, and access to the official records of the association will be filed with the department for mandatory mediation before the dispute is filed in a court. Mediation proceedings must be conducted according to the applicable Florida Rules of Civil Procedure, and these proceedings are privileged and confidential to the same extent as court-ordered mediation. An arbitrator or judge may not consider any information or evidence arising from the mediation proceeding except in a proceeding to impose sanctions for failure to attend a mediation session. Persons who are not parties to the dispute may not attend the mediation conference without the consent of all parties, except for counsel for the parties and a corporate representative designated by the Association. When mediation is attended by a quorum of the board, such mediation is not a board meeting for purposes of notice and participation as defined in Florida Statute 720.303. The department will conduct the proceedings through the use of department mediators or refer the dispute to private mediators who have been duly certified by the department. The parties will share the costs of mediation equally, including the fee charged by the mediator, if any, unless the parties agree otherwise. If a department mediator is used, the department may charge such fees as are necessary to pay expenses of the mediation, including, but not limited to, the salary and benefits of the mediator and any travel expenses incurred. The petitioner will on filing the disputes pay the department a filing fee of $200 to defray the costs of the mediation. At the conclusion of the mediation, the department will charge the parties such further fees as are necessary to fully reimburse the department for all expenses incurred in the mediation; the parties to the mediation will share those fees equally unless otherwise agreed by them.

If the mediation as described above is not successful in resolving all issues between the parties, the parties may file the unresolved dispute in a court of competent jurisdiction or elect to enter into binding or nonbinding arbitration pursuant to the procedures set forth in Florida Statute 718.1255 and rules adopted by the division, with the arbitration proceeding to be conducted by a department arbitrator or by a private arbitrator certified by the department. If all parties do not agree to arbitration proceedings following an unsuccessful mediation, any party may file the dispute in court. A final order resulting from arbitration is final and enforceable in courts if a complaint for trial de novo is not filed in a court of competent jurisdiction within 30 business days after entry of the order.

C) Before UPOAI may seek foreclosure, file suit, charge any fee (including attorneys' fees), limit common area use, or take other action against a homeowner for violation of governing documents, except for an emergency action as provided for below, UPOAI must, in addition to compliance with other law and governing documents, do the following:

1) Provide written notice to the homeowner twice, at least 21 business days apart, that

[a] describes the basis for the claim, including how the homeowner allegedly violated quoted terms of the governing documents;

[b] states the amount claimed due, describes how the homeowner can remedy the violation, confirms the right to comply without waiving the right to dispute the violation, and (where applicable) gives notice of the right to request an installment plan for assessments; and

[c] states that the homeowner has a reasonable period to cure of at least 21 business days after the second notice, unless the homeowner had an opportunity to cure a similar violation within the past six months, and that during the cure

period the homeowner can obtain a hearing as provided in paragraph A-2 above or mediation as provided in paragraph A-3 above, and can contact the Ombudsman, if there is one, without incurring any attorney fees charged by UPOAI; and

2) If the certified mail notice is not delivered, reasonably try to confirm the homeowner's current address and either resend the notice as in paragraph C-1 [a] above or, if no other address can be found, reasonably try to hand-deliver the notice, the period to cure starting anew from this notice.

D) After notice of paragraph C1, homeowners have the right at no cost to a hearing to verify facts and seek resolution with the Directors or a committee designated by the Directors. If the Directors use a committee, any agreement must be enforceable, to be ratified by the Directors unless it conflicts with law or the governing documents, and the homeowner must be allowed to appeal to the Directors or a special meeting of all members. In addition:

1) UPOAI shall hold the hearing within 30 calendar days after receiving the homeowner's request and will provide notice of the date, time and place at least 10 business days before the hearing; the homeowner may request postponement, which will be granted if for not longer than ten business days; additional postponements may be granted by written agreement of the parties; the homeowner may record the meeting; and the committee (and, on any appeal, the Directors) will issue a written decision including the notice required by paragraph G; and

2) UPOAI will extend the period to cure under paragraph C1[c] until 15 business days after notice of the written decision by the committee or directors or special meeting of the members, whichever is greater.

E) After notice of C1[a], except with respect to disputes involving only an assessment or small monetary charge (less than $50), homeowners will have the right to one-half day of neutral mediation, with the proceedings to be kept confidential and not admissible in court except as provided by Florida law. The requesting homeowner(s) will pay 50 percent of the mediator's charge and the Association will pay the balance. If the parties agree on a mediator, the Association will extend the period to cure under paragraph C1[c] until 15 business days after the mediation.

F) After receiving notice of a decision under paragraph D, homeowners have the right, within 15 business days, to invoke the procedure of paragraph E. The notice of decision under paragraph D2 will specify this right.

G) During the period to cure as provided in paragraph C, as extended in paragraphs D - F, the Association will not incur an attorney's fee chargeable to the homeowner, and will not take any enforcement action except for emergency action allowed by paragraph K.

H) UPOAI may not sue a homeowner without an authorizing vote by a majority of all Directors and a separate authorizing vote by a supermajority of at least two thirds [2/3] of all homeowners, in compliance with applicable law and governing documents that may set a higher vote of approval or other requirements.

I) Except for an emergency action allowed by paragraph J, the Association must provide distinct written notice at least 15 business days before filing suit against a homeowner, that

1) describes the basis for the suit, including how the homeowner allegedly violated specified terms of the governing documents; and
2) states any amount the Association claims due, describes how the homeowner can cure the violation, and (where applicable) gives notice of the right to request an installment plan for assessments.

J) Nothing precludes UPOAI from seeking a temporary injunction, or taking temporary enforcement action (such as suspension of rights to use common property), in a good faith response to an emergency. An emergency is a situation that could not have been reasonably foreseen, poses a significant and immediate threat to the community, and makes compliance with the preceding paragraphs impractical. Any temporary enforcement action entitles the homeowner to immediate notice and the related rights above, provided enforcement action may remain in place pending

> 1) the final determination of homeowner rights, or

> 2) the end of the conditions resulting in the immediate and significant threat, whichever comes sooner.

K) Utopia POAI may not charge homeowners for exercise of the foregoing rights but may offer additional options for alternative dispute resolution [ADR]; provided it does not require forbidding ADR, otherwise require a homeowner to waive the right to go to court, or bill homeowners for mandatory ADR. In any litigation, if a party moves to compel nonbinding ADR, the court may consider the extent to which the parties already have pursued ADR.

L) Once each year, UPOAI will alert homeowners by written notice of their rights to ADR, including statutory rights and any others available under these paragraphs.

Section 4. Enforcement. - - Enforcement of these covenants and restrictions will be by a proceeding at law or in equity if and only if all available alternative dispute resolution measures, such as those described above, have been exhausted. In that event a proceeding in law or equity may be brought against any person or persons violating or attempting to violate any covenant or restriction, either to restrain violation or to recover damages, and against the land to enforce any lien created by these covenants. Failure to enforce any covenant or restriction herein contained will in no event be deemed a waiver by any party of the right to do so thereafter. Enforcement may be by Utopia POA, Inc. or by any group of ten (10) or more Owners and should the party seeking enforcement be the prevailing party, then the party against whom enforcement has been sought will pay reasonable attorneys' fees and costs at all trial and appellate levels to the prevailing party.

Section 5. Severability. - - Invalidation of any one of these covenants or restrictions by judgment or court order will in no way affect any other provisions which will remain in full force and effect.

Section 6. Subdivision Use Restrictions. - - Subdivision use restrictions may be filed in connection with any plat of all or any part of Utopia provided they do not conflict with the provisions hereof.

Section 7. Effective Date. - - This Utopia Declaration will become effective upon its recordation in the Public Records of Conch County, Florida.

Section 8. Amendments. - - An Amendment (or amendments) to this Utopia Declaration may not be proposed by the Utopia Board. Amendments to this Declaration may only arise from the process described above dealing with change.

A) Any proposed amendment(s) must be approved in accordance with the process detailed in Article 4 Section 9 above. Each Lot will be entitled to at least one vote by its Owner(s).

B) After approval, the amendment(s) will be transcribed and certified by the President and Secretary as having been duly adopted, and the original or an executed copy of such certified amendment(s) will be recorded in the Public Records of Conch county, Florida, within ten (10) business days from the date on which it or they became effective. The amendment(s) will specifically refer to the numerical recording data uniquely identifying this Utopia Declaration. Thereafter, a copy of the amendment(s) in the form in which the same were placed of record by the officers will be delivered to all of the Members of Utopia POA, Inc., but delivery of a copy thereof will not be a condition precedent to the effectiveness of such amendment(s). At any meeting held to consider such amendment(s), the written vote or votes of any Member of Utopia POA, Inc. will be recognized if the Member is not in attendance at the meeting provided that the Member is represented thereat by proxy, and further provided such written votes are delivered to the Secretary at or prior to such meeting. However, no amendment will reduce the maintenance provisions of this instrument below that required by the Conch county Subdivision and Platting Regulation Ordinance in effect as of September 30, 1978.

C) Any amendment to this Declaration which would affect the lien, security or value of security of any institutional first mortgagee, or the salability of a first mortgage on the secondary market, requires the written joinder and consent of the institutional first mortgagee(s).

Section 9. Prohibited Clauses in Governing Documents. - -

A) Utopia's governing documents, including its disclosure summary, declarations of maintenance covenants, articles of incorporation, or bylaws, may not preclude the display of one portable, removable flag of the United States, any of its armed services, or the official flag of the State of Florida by property owners as long as that flag is:

1) displayed in a respectful manner, consistent with Title 36 U.S.C. chapter 10 and Title 4 chapter 1;

2) not displayed at night or if torn or otherwise damaged or at all above the peak of the roof of the residence where it is displayed;

3) not allowed to touch the ground, and

4) not larger than 4 feet six inches by 6 feet.

B) Utopia's governing documents, including its disclosure summary, declarations of maintenance covenants, articles of incorporation, or bylaws, may not preclude installation of: emergency generators, hurricane shutters, amateur radio antennas, or satellite dishes less than three feet in diameter for noncommercial telecommunications and/or television transmission and/or reception purposes, skylights, or such energy savings devices as: attic fans, roof-mounted solar collectors or solar water heaters or solar cells subject to the following restrictions.

1) The Owner must have made written application to and received written approved from the Architectural Control Committees of Utopia and IDMA including a determination by those committees that the intended device meets county standards and that the installer has all appropriate licenses, insurance and permits to install the device and will display the permit on-site during construction or installation and provide a copy of it to the Association before any work starts.

2) These items must be installed safely and maintained in a safe condition at the owner's expense.

3) Any generator also must be securely anchored to minimize the possibility of theft, and, also at the owner's expense, be made as inconspicuous as possible by use of paint and/or shrubbery and subject to the review and approval of the grounds maintenance committee.

4) Hurricane shutters must match the color of the residence's exterior walls by either original construction or else be painted that color and kept that color at the owner's expense within 30 calendar days of installation unless those shutters are temporary or transparent.

5) Antennas and satellite dishes may not be placed on common ground or in front of a residence or rise more than five feet above the peak of the residence's roof.

6) Anything attached to the side or roof of Utopia dwelling must be able to withstand the winds of a category four hurricane for at least 24 hours.

C) Utopia's governing documents, including its disclosure summary, declarations of maintenance covenants, articles of incorporation, or bylaws, may not prohibit any property owner from implementing Xeriscape — that is, a dry garden of safe materials such as cement, stone and/or sand — or Florida-friendly landscape, as defined in Florida Statute 373.185(1) on his or her land, but not the common ground, after seeking and obtaining written approval of the design from the standing Architectural Control and Grounds Maintenance Committees of Utopia and IDMA and accepting personal responsibility for the cost of maintaining that landscape.

D) Utopia's governing documents, including its disclosure summary, declarations of maintenance covenants, articles of incorporation, or bylaws, may not prohibit any property owner from constructing an access ramp for a resident or occupant of the parcel who has a medical necessity or disability that requires a ramp for egress and ingress under the following conditions:

   1) The ramp must be as unobtrusive as possible, be designed to blend in as aesthetically as possible, and be reasonably sized for its intended use.

   2) Plans for the ramp must be submitted in advance to the Association. The Association may make reasonable requests to modify the design to achieve architectural consistency with the surrounding structures and surfaces.

   3) The parcel owner must submit to the Association an affidavit from a physician attesting to the medical necessity or disability of the resident of the parcel requiring the access ramp. Certification used for Florida statute 320.0848 will be sufficient to meet the affidavit requirement.

E) Display of a Sign. - - Any parcel owner may display a warning sign of reasonable size provided by a contractor for security services within ten (10) feet of any entrance to his home. Reasonable in this case means no larger than three by five feet. However, some other signs are banned including, but are not limited to, those advertising goods or services of the homeowner or a contractor other than the provider of security services and those promoting or advocating of any religious belief.

Section 10. Right of Security against Foreclosure. - - The Association will not foreclose against a homeowner except for significant unpaid assessments, and any such foreclosure will require judicial review to ensure fairness.

A) Utopia POAI may not foreclosure against a homeowner on any lien unless, in addition to compliance with all other applicable laws, the Association obtains a court order that specifies the assessments due, confirms that the Association followed proper procedure, and allows at least three months before the sale date for the homeowner to pay the court-specified debt.

B) UPOAI may not seek an order to foreclose against a homeowner on any lien unless, in addition to compliance with all other laws governing foreclosure of a mortgage on residential real estate,

- 1) the lien secures only a debt for an assessment authorized on a declaration recorded before the homeowner bought the home,

- 2) the Directors by a two-thirds vote and the homeowners by a separate two-thirds vote approve the foreclosure action, and

- 3) the assessment past due on the date of the vote exceeds the greater of $25,000 or 25% of the estimated price of the residence, based on a mean average of at least three independent realtors' estimates.

Notwithstanding the foregoing, any lawfully recorded lien (including liens that do not provide a suitable basis for foreclosure) may be enforced on conveyance of any interest in a home, including conveyance by otherwise proper foreclosure sale.

C) Homeowners have the right to make payments that ensure the following:

- 1) Homeowners may at any time make full or partial payment on any amount due. Any homeowner payment will be credited first toward any past due assessment or other amount due to avoid foreclosure.

2) At least for homeowners who suffer job loss, disability, divorce, or family medical expenses, the Association will without a penalty allow a homeowner 30 business days after an assessment to propose an installment plan. On receiving the homeowner's installment proposal, the Directors will designate a committee to meet with the homeowner privately, and the Association will provide a written response to the homeowner. If the Association does not approve the request in full, the response will allow the homeowner at least 15 business days after denying the request to pay without incurring attorney fees. Nothing prohibits the Directors from approving an installment plan more lenient than provided by existing rules, in which case the existing rules will be amended according to the process set forth elsewhere in these governing documents so that all homeowners will receive fair and equal treatment.

3) Within in five business days after any vote to seek foreclosure, the Association will give the affected homeowner notice of the vote and foreclosure filing.

4) If a homeowner pays all overdue assessments after the Directors and members properly vote to seek foreclosure, a court order nonetheless may permit foreclosure if the homeowner has not paid all overdue late charges plus all attorney fees actually and reasonably incurred after the votes.

5) On a homeowner's request, within three business days, the Association will provide the amount due to avoid foreclosure, including past due assessments and any other amounts allowed by paragraph C4 or approved by court order under paragraph A of this section.

D) Except to the extent that these governing documents provide greater rights elsewhere, after a foreclosure sale by the Association the homeowner has

    1) a right of redemption not less than if a secured lender foreclosed; and

    2) at least 180 business days after recording of notice under paragraph C2, to redeem the home.

Section 11. Right to Fairness in Litigation. - - Where there is litigation between the Association and a homeowner, and the homeowner prevails, the Association will pay attorney fees to a reasonable level.

A) Individual homeowners may sue the Association to enforce statutory rights as well as their rights under these governing documents, without being required to sue other homeowners; further, the Association will pay for any notice to homeowners that the court finds to be appropriate. These governing documents will not limit judicial review or court enforcement; provided they may require ADR to the extent permitted elsewhere in these documents.

B) Unless otherwise provided by statute, a homeowner has the burden to prove each breach of duty by a preponderance of the evidence. Except for ultra vires actions, or actions otherwise exceeding the Association's or Director's authority, homeowners must prove a breach caused, or threatens to cause, injury either to the homeowner as an individual or to the interests of any party of the common-interest community.

C) Homeowner compliance with the Association's demand for action, or demand to cease action, including (but not limited to) any demand to pay assessments or attorney fees, does not waive homeowner rights to challenge such demand.

D) In any case brought by the Association or homeowner to enforce governing documents or applicable law, the homeowner will be awarded reasonable attorney fees and costs to the extent that the homeowner prevails. Attorney fees will reflect counsel's reasonable hourly rate and time worked, and will not be limited by the amount the homeowner actually paid, if any.

E) In any case brought by the Association or homeowner to enforce these governing documents or applicable law, the Association will be awarded reasonable attorney fees and costs to the extent that the Association prevails; provided that the reasonable attorney fees may be reduced at the discretion of the court based on a finding that the judicial review benefitted the Association or homeowners by clarifying these governing documents or applicable law, or other equitable considerations. Attorney fees will reflect counsel's reasonable hourly rate and time worked, limited by the amount the Association actually paid.

Section 12. Right to Be Told of All Rules and Charges. -- The Utopia Property Owners Association, Inc. [UPOAI] may not enforce charges or other rules against homeowners, except those set forth in plain English in its governing documents. All operating rules must be compiled in a single document, available to homeowners on request.

    A) Unless otherwise provided by statute, the following provisions apply:

        1) At least 14 business days before an offer to buy a home becomes binding, the homeowner will furnish the potential buyer with

            [a] the information statement prepared by the Association (including an acknowledgment for the buyer to execute) and all the Association's governing documents, excluding plats and plans;

            [b] a statement of each existing assessment, any unpaid assessment currently due from the selling homeowner, and any other alleged violation of the Association's governing documents by external features of the home or landscape as of the date of the certificate, citing applicable rules;

[c] the Association's current operating budget and financial statement, including any legally required summary of the Association's reserves; and

[d] a statement of the number of foreclosure lawsuits filed within the past three years, any unsatisfied judgments and any pending legal actions against the Association or otherwise relating to the common-interest community of which the homeowner has actual knowledge.

2) On a homeowner's request, within ten business days the Association will furnish a certificate with the information specified in paragraph A1. A requesting homeowner is not liable for erroneous information in the certificate. A buyer is not liable for any past assessment, any future assessment greater than stated in the certificate (unless lawfully increased after the sale), or for violations of governing documents by external features of the home or landscape not stated in the certificate. For this certificate, the Association may charge only actual costs, not to exceed $50.

3) On request by a homeowner, potential buyer in receipt of a certificate pursuant to paragraph A-2, or homeowner's or buyer's authorized agent, within 14 business days the Association will make any legally required study of the Association's reserves reasonably available to copy and/or audit.

B) Governing documents, and statutes governing homeowners, will be construed to favor homeowners' free and unrestricted use of their home, and against any person seeking to enforce a limit on homeowner rights.

1) Absent specific authorization in this Declaration of Maintenance Covenants or in paragraphs B-2 or B-3, UPOAI does not have power to adopt any rules that restrict the use or occupancy of, or behavior within, individually owned homes.

2) Except as limited by statute or these governing documents, UPOAI has implied power to adopt reasonable operating rules to govern the use of

   [a] common property and
   [b] individually owned property to protect the common property.

3) This Declaration grants a general power to adopt rules so that UPOAI also has power to adopt reasonable operating rules designed to

   [a] protect homeowners from unreasonable interference in the enjoyment of their individual homes and the common property cause by use of other individually owned homes; and

   [b] restrict the leasing of homes to meet valid underwriting requirements of institutional lenders.

4) Except to the extent provided by statute or authorized by these governing documents, UPOAI may not impose restrictions on the structures or landscaping that may be placed on individually owned property, or on the design, materials, colors, or plants that may be used.

5) UPOAI may borrow money subject to limits stated in these governing documents but, unless the Declaration or a court-approved order grants specific authority, the Association may not assign future revenues or create a security interest in common property without approval of a supermajority of all homeowners in a vote after at least 30-business-days notice. For the first five years after these documents are recorded that supermajority will be 82%; thereafter the requisite supermajority will decrease in steps of 5% for each

subsequent five-year interval after recording until it falls to 67%; thereafter the required supermajority will remain at two-thirds (2/3).

Section 13. Right to Stability in Rules and Charges. - - Homeowners will have rights to vote to create, amend or terminate deed restrictions and other important documents. The homeowners will have notice and opportunity, by majority or supermajority vote to override any new rules and/or charges.

A) In resolving any conflict among governing documents, the senior document controls. Unless the documents otherwise provide, seniority is:

1) declaration of maintenance covenants over
2) articles of incorporation or association over
3) bylaws over
4) operating rules.

B) The following apply to all governing documents:

1) Except as limited by the governing document, a senior document, or statute, homeowners have the power to amend subject to the following requirements:

[a] unless the governing document, a senior document, or statute specifies a different number, an amendment adopted by homeowners holding a majority of the voting power is effective to

[1] extend the term of the governing document,

[2] make administrative changes reasonably necessary for management of the common property or administration of the servitude regime, or

[3] prohibit or materially restrict uses of individually owned homes that threaten to harm or unreasonably interfere with reasonable use and enjoyment of other

property in the community, or to amend or repeal such prohibition or restriction adopted by amendment under this paragraph B-1[a][3].

[b] Unless the governing document, a senior document or statute specifies a different number, an amendment adopted by homeowners holding two-thirds of the voting power is effective for all other lawful purposed except as stated in paragraphs B2 and B3.

2) Amendments that do not apply uniformly to similar homes and amendments that would violate Association duties to homeowners under the law and/or these governing documents are not effective without unanimous approval by homeowners whose interests would be adversely affected, unless the declaration clearly and specifically apprises purchasers that such amendments may be made. Paragraph B2 does not apply to non-uniform modifications made under circumstances that would justify judicial modification.

3) Except as otherwise expressly authorized by these governing documents, and except as provided in paragraph B1, unanimous homeowner approval is required to:

[a] prohibit or materially restrict use of occupancy of, or behavior within individually owned lots or units, or

[b] change the basis for allocating voting rights or assessments among homeowners.

4) At least 60 business days before voting on any proposed amendment to a governing document, the Association will provide notice to all homeowners, including the specific text proposed and a description of the amendment's purpose and anticipated effects. No amendment takes effect before the Association provides notice of adoption to all homeowners, certified

by an Association officer, and to the extent required by law, the Association records the amendment.

5) Directors have no power to amend a governing document except where expressly authorized by the governing document or a senior document; provided that, if governing documents authorize Directors to impose any duty or charge on homeowners, this will be done by operating rule (as provided in paragraph C) unless the governing document requires otherwise; and provided further that homeowners only, not Directors, will have power to amend

> [a] any provision that affects number, qualifications, powers and duties, terms of office, or manner and time or election or removal of Directors; or
>
> [b] any provision with respect to amendment of any governing document.

C) Directors may adopt, amend, or repeal operating rules if and only if all of the following requirements are satisfied:

1) All operating rules must be

> [a] in writing;
>
> [b] within Directors' authority conferred by law or these governing documents;
>
> [c] consistent with law and these governing documents;
>
> [d] adopted, amended, or repealed in good faith and in substantial compliance with law and these governing documents; and
>
> [e] reasonable.

2) Paragraphs C4 and C5 apply only to operating rules that relate to one or more of the following subjects:

[a] Use of common property;

[b] Use of a home, including any aesthetic or architectural standards that govern the alteration of a home;

[c] Homeowner discipline, including any withdrawal of privileges or charges for violating governing documents and any procedure for withdrawing privileges or imposing charges;

[d] Any standard for delinquent assessment installment or other payment plans;

[e] Any procedure to resolve disputes;

[f] Any procedure for reviewing and approving or disapproving a proposed physical change to a home or to the common area; and/or

[g] Any procedure for elections.

3) For the following actions by Directors, paragraphs C4 and C5 do not apply:

[a] A decision regarding maintenance of the common property;

[b] A decision on a specific matter that is not intended to apply generally;

[c] A decision setting the amount of a regular or special assessment;

[d] A rule change required by law, if Directors have no discretion as to the substantive effect of the rule change; and/or

[e] Issuance of a document that merely repeats existing laws or the governing documents.

4) Directors will provide written notice of a proposed rule change to homeowners at least 30 business days before voting on the rule change. The notice shall included the text, and a description of the purpose and effect of the proposed rule change, except as provided by paragraph C4[c].

> [a] A decision to recommend a proposed rule change for approval or rejection by the general membership shall be made at a meeting of the Directors but only after consideration of any comments made by homeowners.
>
> [b] Nor more than 15 calendar days after approving the rule change for consideration by the Members, the Directors will deliver notice of the proposed rule change to every homeowner. If the rule change is an emergency rule change made under paragraph C4[c], the notice will include the text of the rule change, a description of the purpose and effect of the rule change, and the date that the rule change expires.
>
> [c] If Directors determine that an immediate rule change is required to address an imminent threat to public health or safety or an imminent risk of substantial economic loss to the Association, Directors may make an emergency rule change; and no prior notice is required. An emergency rule change is effective for 120 calendar days, unless the rule change provides for a shorter effective period. A rule change made under this paragraph C4[c] may not be readopted under this paragraph.

5) Homeowners holding five (5) percent of the voting power may call a special meeting of the homeowners to reverse any rule change.
> [a] To call such a special meeting homeowners must, no more than 30 business days after being notified of a rule change, deliver a written

request to the Association's president, secretary, or registered agent, after which the Directors will give notice of the meeting to all homeowners. Homeowners are deemed notified of a rule change after receiving notice of the rule change or enforcement of the resulting rule, whichever happens first. Homeowner requests to copy or review Association member lists with addresses, e-mail, and phone numbers for the purpose of seeking support to reverse a rule change will be honored as soon as reasonably possible, in any event within three business days. Homeowners will be allowed to use common property reasonably in seeking support to reverse a rule change.

[b] At such a special meeting with a quorum present, the rule change will be reversed by majority vote of homeowners represented and voting, unless these governing documents or statute requires otherwise.

[c] Unless otherwise provided by these governing documents, for this paragraph C5, one vote may be cast for each home.

[d] Special meetings under this paragraph C5 will follow laws generally applicable to special meetings.

[e] A rule change reversed under this paragraph C5 may not be readopted for three years after the date of the meeting reversing the rule change. Nothing in this paragraph C5 precludes Directors from considering adopting a different rule on the same subject as a rule change that has been reversed.

[f] As soon as possible and not more than 15 calendar days after the close of voting at a special meeting, the Directors will provide every homeowner with notice of the results of a vote held pursuant to this paragraph C5.

[g] This paragraph C5 does not apply to emergency rule changes under paragraph C4[c].

D) Unless elsewhere within these governing documents a longer period is required, homeowner votes to impose or increase regular or special assessments require at least 30 business-days advance notice.

Section 14. Right to Individual Autonomy. - - Homeowners will not surrender any essential rights of individual autonomy because they live in a common-interest community. Homeowners have the right to peaceful advocacy during elections and other votes as well as use of common areas.

A) Homeowners have the right to display noncommercial signs, flags, and for sale signs on their property, provided the Declaration may set reasonable limits so long as, for three months before any election or other vote held by the Association or a government or other entity with geographic territory overlapping any part of the common-interest community, the Association will not forbid display of reasonable-size signs relating to the election or vote. See Section 9 above for restrictions on flags and signs.

B) Homeowners have the right to peacefully visit, telephone, petition, or otherwise contact their neighbors; provided the Declaration may set reasonable restrictions if it permits some weekday afternoon and some weekend hours for such neighbor contacts.

C) Homeowners have the right to invite guests to assemble peacefully on their property, provided the Declaration may set reasonable limits to protect nearby homes.

D) Where the Association makes any part of the common property available for use by homeowners:

1) the governing documents will state any charge for homeowners' use, which will not exceed the Association's marginal cost for use, as well as any other restrictions on such use, which will be content-neutral and otherwise reasonable; and

2) the governing documents will not unreasonably restrict homeowners' rights to invite public officers or candidates for public office to appear or speak in common areas, or unreasonably restrict lawful uses relating to an election or other vote held by the Association or any government or quasi-governmental entity with geographic territory overlapping any part of the common-interest community.

E) Restrictions on signs and flags, neighbor contacts, peaceful assembly, common property, or other self-expression will not differ based on the content of a view sought to be expressed by a homeowner. If the Association allows homeowners to express views on a topic, in a newsletter or other forum, other homeowners equally will be allowed to respond with differing views.

F) UPOAI may not force a homeowner to join a separate organization, such as a country club, unless

1) expressly authorized by the Declaration before the homeowner's purchase, which this Declaration does not, or

2) associations merge in compliance with state law.

G) Assessments of mandatory dues from Association members may not be used by the Association for charitable or political purposes. Any solicitations for charitable or political purposes by the Association will be conducted separately from the billing or customary assessments of fees, and clearly be designated as voluntary.

H) The governing documents must be created in compliance with law, and not include terms that are illegal or unconstitutional, or that violate public policy. Terms that are invalid because they violate public policy include, but are not limited to, terms that:

1) are arbitrary, spiteful, or capricious;
2) unreasonably burden a fundamental constitutional right;
3) impose an unreasonable restraint on alienation;
4) impose an unreasonable restraint on trade or competition; or
5) are unconscionable.

Section 15. Right to Oversight of the Association and Directors. - - Homeowners will have reasonable access to records and meetings, as well as specified abilities to call special meetings, to obtain oversight of elections and other votes, and to recall Directors.

A) All Association meeting minutes, financial and budget materials, contracts, court filings, and other records must be maintained for at least seven years at the Association's main business office or other suitable location near homes in the Association.

1) Except as provided in paragraph A2, the Association must make all records available for homeowners, their authorized agents, or the Ombudsman, if one exists, to inspect and copy

[a] during regular working hours, within ten business days of a written request without requiring a statement of purpose or reason; and

[b] during an inspection, allowing copying of up to 25 pages at no cost, if the Association or its agent has a photocopy machine at the site of the records; and in any event

[c] with a charge to the homeowner only for actual copying costs incurred by the Association, not to exceed twice the going local commercial rate plus staff time charges not to exceed the minimum wage plus $2.00 per hour. The Association may not impose charges for copies

made by digital cameras, portable scanners, or other equipment homeowners themselves provide.

2) Documents protected by the attorney-client privilege or as work product are exempt from disclosure to the same extent as they would be in litigation, as are contracts being negotiated. The following records also are exempt from disclosure to homeowners or their agents, except on court order for good cause shown, provided that the Ombudsman may obtain the following records, and provided further that such records will be kept confidential except on court order for good cause shown:

> [a] staff personnel records, except the Association will make available under paragraph A1 records of time worked and salary and benefits paid; and
>
> [b] records of homeowners other than the requester, except the Association will make available under paragraph A1 the list of homeowners with their mailing addresses and a compilation of violations of the governing documents, other than for nonpayment of an assessment, and this compilation must
>
>> [1] describe the violation alleged and the sanction sought or imposed; and
>> [2] not identify the person against whom the sanction was sought unless the matter was considered in an open meeting or court.

3) if the Association refuses to allow a homeowner, homeowner's agent, or the Ombudsman, if there is one, to review records as provided herein, the requester is entitled to an immediate injunction, a penalty of $500, or in the court's discretion, more, and attorney fees, even if the Association makes records available after filing a case.

4) Any Director may inspect any Association records, except attorney-client privileged or work product records concerning potential, ongoing, or past litigation against the Director. In addition to their rights under paragraph A1, Directors may make copies of minutes of any meeting during their term of office, and of any other document for purposes reasonably related to their duties as Directors. Pending litigation does not reduce the rights provided in this paragraph.

B) Every 90 calendar days (or more frequently if required elsewhere in these governing documents), the Directors will review at one of the Association's meetings

1) the latest statement from financial institutions that hold Association accounts;
2) current reconciliations of the Association's operating and reserve accounts;
3) year-to-year income and expense statement for Association operating accounts, compared to the budget;
4) year-to-year revenues and expenses for the reserve amount(s), compared with the budget; and
5) the status of any lawsuit, arbitration, or mediation involving the Association.

C) Except for executive sessions as defined in paragraph 1 below, homeowners may attend, record, and (subject to reasonable limits) speak at any meeting of the Association or its Directors.

1) Directors may meet in executive session only to:

[a] approve, modify, terminate or take other action regarding a contract between the Association and an attorney;
[b] consult with counsel on litigation or otherwise to obtain legal advice, if the discussion would be protected by attorney-client privilege;
[c] discuss the character, alleged misconduct, professional competence, or physical or mental health of an Association manager or employee;

[d] discuss a homeowner's failure to pay an assessment or other alleged violation of governing documents, except as provided in paragraph C2; or

[e] discuss ongoing contract negotiations.

2) Directors will only use an executive session to discuss alleged violations of governing documents unless the person who may be sanctioned requests an open meeting in writing. The person who may be sanctioned must be notified in writing of the session at least 30 calendar days in advance, may attend and testify at any portion of the session concerning the alleged violation, but has no right to attend Director deliberations.

3) Meeting minutes will note generally any matter discussed in an executive session.

D) All votes by Directors will be recorded in the minutes available to all homeowners, except to the extent permitted in paragraph C. Directors may not vote by proxy or by secret ballot, except a secret ballot to elect officers. This rule applies to any committee or agent of the Association that makes final decisions to spend Association funds, or approve or disapprove architectural decisions.

E) In addition to any provisions for special meetings elsewhere in these governing documents, the following provisions apply:

1) The Directors will provide 30 business days notice and convene a special meeting of the Association to be held no less than 30 business days and no more than 90 business days after the chair, the secretary, or the Association's registered agent receives a petition stating one or more purposes for such meeting and signed by homeowners holding 10 percent of the voting power, unless other law or these governing documents elsewhere state a different percentage.

2) The petition may specify a person to chair the meeting

and that person need not be a Member, Director or officer of the Association.

3) Each purpose and, if specified in the petition, the chair of such special meeting will be stated in its notice.

4) Failure of the Directors to provide notice and convene the meeting as provided in paragraph E1 automatically invalidates any and all actions taken by the Directors at that and all subsequent board meetings.

F) Directors will be subject to recall (with or without the use of proxy votes) as follows:

1) Any Director may be recalled without cause by persons holding a majority of the total voting power, provided a homeowner's voting power for purposes of recall equals that to elect Directors, and when only specific homeowners have power to elect a Director, only those homeowners have voting power for recall.

2) One or more Directors may be recalled by written agreement or ballots without an annual or special meeting.

[a] The written agreement or ballots, or a copy thereof, will be served on the Association by certified mail or by personal service under process permitted by state law.

[b] Within five business days after receipt of the agreement or ballots, the Directors will meet — without excluding Directors proposed for recall — and, as the only business as to each Director proposed for recall will either:

[1] certify the recall, in which case the recall takes effect immediately and the recalled Director will within five business days turn over to the Association all Association records and property possessed by the Director, or

[2] proceed as described in paragraph F4 below.

[3] If a court finds a recall effort defective, written recall agreements or ballots used in that recall effort and not found defective may be reused in only the next recall effort, if any. However, no written recall agreement or ballot will be valid more than 120 business days after being signed by a homeowner.

[4] A homeowner may revoke a vote by recall agreement or ballot, but only in writing delivered to the Association before service of the recall agreement or ballot.

3) Homeowners may recall a Director or Directors by a vote taken at an annual or special meeting of homeowners.

[a] A special meeting of homeowners to recall a Director of Directors may be called by homeowners with 15 percent of voting power (as defined in paragraph F1) by giving notice as required for a special meeting, except that electronic transmissions may not be used, and the notice will state the purpose of the meeting.

[b] Within five business days after the special meeting, the Directors shall meet — without excluding all Directors proposed for recall — and, as their only business, as to each Director proposed for recall Will either

[1] certify the vote to recall, in which case recall takes effect immediately and the recalled Director will within five business days turn over to the Association all Association records and property possessed by the Director, or

[2] proceed as described in paragraph F4 just below.

4) Separately with respect to each Director proposed for recall, if the Directors do not certify the recall, the Directors will, within five business days after their meeting, petition the DPBR for arbitration, following procedures adopted by the DPBR. For purposes of this arbitration homeowners who voted for the recall will be considered one party under the petition. If the arbitrator certifies the recall of a Director, the recall will be effective on mailing the final order of arbitration to the Association, and each Director so recalled will deliver to the Association all records and property of the Association possessed by the Director within five business days after notice of the recall. Such decision will be subject to review in court with jurisdiction in the county where the Association maintains its principal office, but such pending action will not delay implementation of the arbitrator's decision.

5) Vacancies created by recall will be filled by homeowner vote held within 30 business days after the recall is certified by the Directors or by the Ombudsman, except that a Director whose term expires within 30 business days need not be replaced, provided

[a] for recall pursuant to paragraph F2 above, no separate vote will be held if the written agreement or ballot specifies one replacement Director for each Director recalled; and homeowners holding a majority of the voting power vote for the named replacements; and

[b] for recall pursuant to paragraph F3 above, the homeowner vote for replacement may take place at the same meeting held for the recall.

6) If the Directors fail to meet within five business days after service of a written recall agreement or ballot pursuant to paragraph F2, or within five business days after adjournment of a recall meeting pursuant to

paragraph F3, the recall will be deemed effective and the Directors so recalled will immediately turn over to the Association all records and property of the Association. Any homeowner may petition the DPBR for certification that Directors have been recalled pursuant to this paragraph F6.

7) If a Director who is removed fails to relinquish office or turn over records and property as required under this paragraph F, a court in the county where the Association maintains its principal office may, on the petition by the Association, or homeowners, summarily order the Director to relinquish office and turn over all Association records, property and documents to the Association.

8) Minutes of the meeting where Directors decide whether to certify the recalls are an Association record. The minutes must record the date and time, each decision, and the vote count taken separately as to each Director proposed for recall. In addition, where the Directors decide not to certify a recall, as to each rejected recall, the minutes must identify any rejected vote and the specific reason for each such rejection.

9) When recall of more than one Director is sought, the written agreement, ballot, or vote at a meeting will provide for a separate vote for each Director sought to be recalled.

10) Nothing in this paragraph F prevents a recalled Director from retaining documents lawfully obtained under paragraph A.

Section 16. Right to Vote and Run for Office. - - Homeowners will have well-defined voting rights and no Director will have a conflict of interest.

A) UPOAI may not deny a homeowner's right to vote on any issue that affects an assessment or other provision of governing documents that apply to the membership.

1) For a home with multiple owners, the owners must file a certificate with the Association designating a specific individual to vote for them as provided for elsewhere in these documents.

2) No vote may be cast except by the homeowner or her/his duly authorized agent, provided the following applies in addition to any other requirements stated elsewhere in these governing documents.

[a] The proxy must be dated and designate a meeting for which it applies.

[b] The proxy may not be revocable without notice, and may be revoked only by actual written notice to the person presiding over the meeting.

[c] A proxy is presumed to grant the designated agent full discretion to act unless it designated each specific agenda item to which it applies and tells the agent how to deal with that item. A homeowner may execute a proxy without designating any item to be used solely to determine whether a quorum exists. For each specific agenda item designated the proxy must specify a vote for or against the proposition or, in an election or recall, state a specific position regarding whom to vote for or whether to vote for or against recall. If a proxy does not state explicit instructions to vote on an item, the agent must be treated as if the homeowner were present and voting on that item.

[d] When an agent casts proxy votes, s/he must disclose the number of proxies held, and the proxies must be kept as part of the public record of the meeting for the period provided by law.

[e] UPOAI's governing documents provide for a homeowner or her/his agent voting in person or by absentee ballot, with the ballot as specific as any other proxy, and with the Association's

secretary to announce the number of such ballots received for each vote at the meeting, and the ballots kept as part of the public record of the meeting.

    3) Votes allocated to homes owned by the Association may not be cast, by proxy or otherwise, for any purpose.

B) No homeowner may be denied the right to run for office provided s/he meets the eligibility standards set forth below and elsewhere in these governing documents.

    1) A person may not serve as Director or officer of an Association if the person or any relative (defined under state law) serves as manager for the Association or as a Director or officer of the Master Association if manager of any Association that is subject to the governing documents of the master association.

    2) Each candidate named on a ballot for Director must make a good faith effort to disclose in writing, by actual notice to all homeowners or as otherwise provided in these governing documents, any financial, business, professional or personal relationship or interest that would appear to a reasonable person to result in a potential conflict of interest if the candidate were elected Director.

C) Unless state law sets different requirements, and if not otherwise specified by these governing documents, a quorum exists if homeowners with 25 percent of voting power attend, or where permitted, are present by proxy at a meeting. At any meeting, election of Directors, recalls, and homeowner votes on assessments, amendment to governing documents, operating rules, or other matters will be conducted by secret ballot (except as provided with respect to proxies in paragraph A2), with all ballots kept as part of the records of the election for the period provided by law.

D) If any candidate for an election, or homeowner advocating a point of view for purposes reasonably related to a homeowner vote, is permitted to use a forum that is paid for by the community (such as a newsletter, bulletin board, or meeting area) to promote his or her candidacy for a board election, then other candidates and homeowners will also be permitted equal access to the same forum under the same conditions.

Section 17. Right to Reasonable Association and Directors. - - The Association, its directors, and their other agents will act reasonably in exercising their power over homeowners.

A) In addition to compliance with law and these governing documents, the Association (whether through Directors, officers, managers, or other agents, by homeowner vote, or otherwise) has the following duties to its homeowners:

   1) To use the extraordinary care and prudence of a fiduciary in managing property and financial affairs;
   2) To treat homeowners fairly; and
   3) To act reasonably in the exercise of discretionary powers, including rulemaking, enforcement, and design control powers.

B) In addition to compliance with law and these governing documents, Association Directors, officers, managers, and other agents must act in good faith, deal fairly with the Association and its homeowners, and use the extraordinary care and prudence of a fiduciary in performing their functions.

   1) A Director, officer, attorney, manager, or other agent of the Association will not solicit or accept any form of compensation, gratuity or other remuneration that

      [a] would improperly influence or would appear to a reasonable person to improperly influence the decisions made by such agent; or
      [b] would result or would appear to a reasonable person to result in a conflict of interest for such agent.

2) A Director or an officer of the Association will not:

    [a] enter into or renew a contract with the Association to provide goods or services to the Association; or

    [b] otherwise accept any commission, personal profit, or compensation of any kind from the Association for providing goods or services to the Association.

C) In contracting for a lawyer to seek foreclosure or take other enforcement action, the Association may not make legal fees in whole or part contingent on the amount paid (for fees or otherwise) by a homeowner. Any homeowner payment to the lawyer will be held for the Association. No contract may authorize anyone to prevent a homeowner from seeking to resolve any dispute directly with Directors or other agents of the Association.

D) All Association managers must be licensed and bonded where required by law. In contracting with managers, the Association may pay a flat fee, hourly rates, or a combination of flat fees and hourly rates. Managers may not be paid any fee, bonus, incentive, or other amount based on the number or value of violations they allege or address. Managers may not impose charges on homeowners, except where reasonable and expressly authorized by these governing documents. All homeowner payments to the manager will be held for the Association.

E) A homeowner's request that the Association or related architectural body approve the homeowner's planned construction, landscaping, maintenance, or repairs will be deemed approved unless, within 30 business days or such other period as the Declaration may specify, the Association or architectural body provides written notice specifically detailing a lawful basis for disapproval in whole or part. Such notice will specify that homeowners have the right to reconsideration by the Directors, unless the Directors collectively made the original decision. Each year the Association will remind homeowners in writing that rules govern approval of construction, landscaping, maintenance, or repairs.

F) Fines and other charges:

1) Where otherwise authorized by the statute, the Association may seek a court order to impose fines for a homeowner's willful noncompliance with duties under these governing documents, but may not otherwise impose fines.

2) Where authorized by these governing documents, the Association may recover reasonable compensation for damages or costs (such as late fees) when a homeowner's rule breaking actually harms the Association; provided that the Association cannot place a lien for such charges without a court judgment.

3) Nothing here prevents the Association from withdrawing homeowners' privileges to use recreational and social facilities where otherwise authorized, including withdrawal for nonpayment of fines or other charges authorized in this paragraph F.

G. Retaliation is specifically forbidden. The Association, its Directors, officers, manager or other agent of the Association may not take, or direct, or encourage another person to attempt retaliatory action against a homeowner because the homeowner has:

1) complained about alleged violations of law or governing documents;

2) requested to review books, records, or other papers of the Association; or

3) taken any other lawful action asserting homeowner rights or otherwise seeking to improve Association operations.

The forbidden retaliatory action includes, without limitation, ill-motivated litigation (for example, Strategic Lawsuits Against Public Participation, or SLAPP suits) as well as deprivation of other rights protected by law or these governing documents.

H) In addition to other remedies authorized by law, homeowners are entitled to recover compensatory damages and, for intentional violations, punitive damages from the Association, and its Directors, officers, managers, or other agents who act unlawfully. In addition, on proof of intentional violations by Directors, officers, managers, or other agents of the Association, homeowners are entitled to appropriate relief in equity including (without limitation) removal of offenders from positions with the Association, a bar against their return to office for a specified time, and an order requiring the offender to repay the Association for expenses including legal fees. The attorney general (and if otherwise authorized, local government officials) may obtain the same relief as any other homeowner as well as any other appropriate equitable relief including a bar against the offender's serving in any capacity for an association.

Section 18. Declaration of Covenants: Survival after Tax Deed or Foreclosure. - - All provisions of this declaration of covenants relating to a parcel that has been sold for taxes or special assessments survive and are enforceable after the issuance of a tax deed, or on the foreclosure of an assessment, a certificate or lien, a tax deed, tax certificate, or tax lien, to the same extent that they would be enforceable against a voluntary grantee of title to the parcel immediately before the delivery of the tax deed or immediately before the foreclosure.

Section 19. Pets. - - No live animal pets are allowed in Utopia whether kept indoors or not and for any period no matter how brief. Live pets, whether birds, dogs, cats, ferrets, fish, insects, and/or reptiles, are forbidden whether brought into the community permanently or temporarily by a Member, tenant, guest or employee. There are only two exceptions to this prohibition, one is the legal requirement to allow a working seeing-eye dog and the other is noted below.

A) The Board will regularly inspect for pets and has an easement to enter residences with or without advance notice during reasonable hours—that is between 8 a.m. and 9 p.m. — local standard time to inspect for the presence of a pet.

B) If a pet is found during the inspection or otherwise observed in Utopia, the Owner is to be immediately warned in writing to permanently remove it within the next three calendar days and not replace it or face escalating fines and the immediate suspension their right to use the common areas until the pet is removed.

C) Fines for having a pet will start at $10 per pet per day for the first two days after the warning period; then double to $20 per pet per day for the next two days; the fine redoubles to $40 per pet per day for the sixth and seventh days and redoubles again to $80 per pet per day for the eighth and ninth days. The fine will be $100 per pet per day after the ninth day and continues until the pet is permanently removed. If the pet returns or another one is introduced, a warning notice need not be given and the fine will be $100 per pet per day.

D) The Board has the right to enter the premises during reasonable to remove or have the pet(s) removed to an animal shelter of its choice and to bill the Owner for the expenses incurred for doing so if the Owner has not done so within ten (10) calendar days of receiving a written warning to remove the pet.

E) Any pet(s) that can be documented as in place before 2005 may be kept until they die, stray, are given away or sold but may not be replaced.

F) Potential buyers must be notified of the details of this rule during the screening interview and must sign an agreement to obey it as a precondition of purchase.

Section 20. Pool Rules. - - As the pool area is the only significant amenity available to Utopia homeowners and their guests, experience shows that the following rules are essential to promote the safe and equitable use of this key community resource.

A) The pool "area" consists of the space enclosed by hedges, fences, gates and the west wall of the bathhouse which area contains the pool, the deck around the pool including the "patio" between the bathhouse and the pool deck, the adjacent sidewalks, the bathhouse and any attachments thereto.

B) The basic rules for using the pool area are posted at the pool but the following items and clarifications also apply:

    1) prohibitions:

        [a] no smoking in the pool area;
        [b] no private parties or private games of chance;
        [c] no games involving money — no matter how small the sum(s) involved;
        [d] no reserving space for any purpose including meetings or groups of friends and/or relatives; and
        [e] no one incontinent or wearing a diaper can use the pool regardless of their age.

    2) Security is to be called on the phone on the east wall of the bathhouse or otherwise notified immediately of any violation of these prohibitions and must require the offending parties to leave the pool area for the rest of the day. A second violation by the same individual(s) requires barring them and their immediate family and all guests from using the pool area for the next seven consecutive calendar days. Subsequent violations by the same individual will justify more drastic penalties, including fines, and longer suspensions going first to a ban of 14 consecutive calendar days, next a ban of 30 consecutive calendar days, and then a ban for 90 consecutive calendar days.

    3) Showering is required from head to toe, without the use of soap or shampoo, in the bathhouse before entering the pool and before reentering the pool if one leaves the pool for more than ten (10) minutes. Anyone triggering the closing of the pool by the Conch county

authorities for not showering is personally responsible all associated costs including fines and the cost of cleaning and refilling the pool and any documented costs incurred by other residents or their guests in using the alternate pool of their choice as a result of the closing of Utopia's pool. Security is to be called on the phone on the east wall of the bathhouse or otherwise notified immediately of any violation of these prohibitions and must require the offender(s) to leave the pool area for the rest of the day. A second violation by the same individual(s) requires suspending them and their immediate family and all guests from using the pool area for the same periods as in paragraph 2 immediately above.

4) No food or beverages are allowed in the pool area with two exceptions.

[a] One may drink water from the drinking fountain or from clear plastic bottles brought to the pool area provided the latter are taken from the pool area at the end of the drinker's visit to the pool area.

[b] Food and beverages may be served only on paper or plastic plates and in paper or plastic glasses at a social affair open to the entire community and guests of residents if and only if [1] it was previously approved by a resolution of the Board of the Association. [2] the organizers of the affair remove from the pool area all decorations and garbage resulting from the affair as soon as possible after the affair ends, and [3] that no more than four (4) such affairs are held in any calendar year and no more than three (3) in the period from October first through March 31st of consecutive years.

[c] Security is to be called on the phone on the east wall of the bathhouse or otherwise notified immediately of any violation of these

prohibitions and must require the offender(s) to leave the pool area for the rest of the day. A second violation by the same individual(s) requires suspending them and their immediate family and all guests from using the pool area for the same periods as in paragraph 2 above.

5) The pool area may NOT be used between dusk and dawn except in the case of an emergency or for a community wide social affair described above.

6) The pool is closed as soon as practical after dusk and opened as soon as practical after dawn by Security using a chain and a key lock on each gate to the pool area. The key(s) to those locks will be kept in the sole possession of Security rather than any Member(s) of the community. Violation of this rule could compel the Association to not only incur drastically higher insurance fees but also to invest in costly stadium lighting and keep those lights on at night at considerable extra expense.

7) Handicapped individuals may ask the Board for permission to shower at home immediately before using the pool and the Board will look favorably on such requests but need not automatically grant them as Utopia is exempt from making any such accommodations under the American Disability Act.

8) The pool area and in particular the bathhouse and flower beds are to be maintained and repaired so as to stay close as possible to their original design and any approved alterations thereto made before the year 2000.

9) Residents and their guests may use the pool area only during daylight hours and only as long as they obey the rules, act decorously, and are considerate of all other users. Impeding access to or from the bathhouse showers; loud conversations; words or deeds promoting discrimination or apparently discriminatory on the basis of age, color, gender, nationality, occupation,

race, or religion, size or shape, or violence or the threat of violence are so inappropriate that they are punishable by suspension of the right to use the pool area and/or fines.

10) The primary purposes of the mandatory bathhouse are to provide showers and toilets for Members and guests. Anything which may or does interfere with those essential functions of the bathhouse is prohibited.

Section 21. Rules for Working at or from Home in Utopia. -- The Conch county's Zoning Board established rules determining the kinds of work which may or may not be done at or from home in Utopia. Anything not expressly prohibited by those rules, as restated below, is allowed.

A) Number & Kinds of Workers. -- One or more family members may work at home but no more than one person not a member of the immediate family in residence may be employed in the home occupation(s) conducted in the residence.

B) Restrictions on Work at Home. Work at home is permissible if and only if all of the following restrictions are satisfied:

1) The work clearly is incidental and secondary to the residential use of the building and confined to no more than 10% of the total floor area of the dwelling.

2) All proper licenses were obtained, if necessary, and are current.

3) The business is NOT open to the general public, that is, no retailing or on-premises sales.

4) The occupation does not change the essential residential character of the building in terms of exterior appearance and interior space.

5) The home occupation is conducted inside the dwelling — that is, not in any open porch or attached carport or unattached accessory building or structure — unless an outside instructional service.

6) The occupation(s) must not produce noise, electrical or magnetic interference, vibration, heat, glare, smoke, dust, odor or other nuisance outside the residential building. Hazardous or noxious materials may not be stored on-site. No noise of an objectionable nature from the home will be audible at the adjoining property lines.

7) Only one business-related vehicle, other than construction equipment, per dwelling unit may be parked at the home if not over three (3) tons rated capacity; properly registered or licensed; used by a resident of the premises; gross weight does not exceed five (5) tons, including load; height does not exceed nine (9) feet, including any load, bed, or box; and total vehicle length does not exceed 26 feet. Advertising on the vehicle is limited to the minimum to meet code requirements mandated by Conch county Contractors Certification Division.

8) More than one home occupation may be permitted on a residential lot.

9) No advertising or disclosure of the street address of the home occupation through signs, billboards, TV, radio or newspapers is allowed.

Section 22. General Principles for All Meetings. - - The presiding officer at any meeting, whether a Board meeting, a meeting of a Board committee, or a meeting of the Members, is responsible for maintaining an orderly and decorous process. Failure to do so, regardless of the reason(s), is automatic grounds to suspend the presiding officer for breach of her/his fiduciary duty pending an appeal which may lead to declaring the presiding officer immediately and permanently ineligible for service on the Board and its committees.

A) The presiding officer must immediately stop the proceedings to warn any attendee, Director and/or officer whose behavior could tend to disrupt or is disrupting the orderly conduct or decorum of the meeting but may only do so once for each offender. The warning must state that such behavior is inappropriate and will, if continued or repeated in the future, lead to:

1) suspension of the meeting until the offender immediately and publicly either apologizes to the Board and the other attendees and agrees to behave properly or leaves the meeting until s/he controls her/himself;

2) adjournment of the meeting;

3) expulsion from the meeting, if necessary with the aid of Security personnel,

4) barring the offender from personal participation in all future meetings of the Board and membership save by an authorized representative who behaves properly, and

5) the offender being declared immediately and permanently ineligible for service on the Board and any of its committees.

B) Inappropriate behavior by a Director or attendee includes, but is not limited to any individual or group who:

1) talks to others without having the floor while the meeting is in progress;

2) cheers, claps, groans, jeers, whistles, and/or yells or screams;

3) personally insults or threatens another attendee or Director;

4) engages in pettifoggery;

5) advocates, advances or relies on or repeats false, irrational, irrelevant, undocumented, subjective or

impossible to prove arguments such as: we just want to have fun, other communities do or have done it, we are/represent the majority, we know what everyone thinks or will think about ..., who does it hurt?, it'll lower or raise property values, we've gotten away with it before so we can continue to do it, no laws apply inside a gated community, and so forth; or

6) incessantly interrupts the proceedings with comments, questions and/or criticisms.

ARTICLES OF INCORPORATION

OF

UTOPIA POA, INC.

(a corporation not for profit)

ARTICLE 1

Name

The name of this corporation will be UTOPIA POA, INC. (the "Association").

ARTICLE 2

Purposes

The general nature, objects and purposes of the Association are:

Section 1. Promote Property Owners' Health, Safety, and Social Welfare. - - To promote the health, safety and social welfare of the owners of property within that area hereinafter be referred to as Utopia but only in so far as these aims can be objectively measured and tradeoffs made explicitly between them by a valid technique such as Saaty's Analytic Hierarchy Process [Saaty's AHP]. [Saaty's AHP is described in *Decision Making for Leaders* by Thomas Saaty and is available as a book and as a software program from Expert Choice, Inc. of Pittsburgh, PA.]

> A) In the event of a conflict between any two or more goals, safety of the majority takes complete priority over that of an individual or health of the majority or an individual; health of the majority has priority over that of any individual or the social welfare of the majority; and the social welfare of the majority only has priority over the social welfare of any

individual. Moreover, any individual's safety, health or social welfare presumably has the same value as that of any other individual unless a meaningful difference can be objectively established.

B) Protection and/or enhancement of residential property prices or "values," either individually or collectively, is not a Board responsibility and is not acceptable as an argument in support of any proposed change because property prices mostly depend on demand factors which the Board cannot control and has no authority to try.

Section 2. Hold Title to Common Areas. - - To hold title to the Common Areas.

Section 3. Maintenance and Repair. - - To maintain and/or repair landscaping in the general and/or Common Areas, parks, sidewalks and/or access paths, streets, and other Common Areas, structures, and other improvements in Utopia for which the obligation to maintain and repair has been delegated and accepted.

Section 4. Architectural Control. - - To control, subject to the provisions of the Declaration of Maintenance Covenants of Illyrian Dales Master Association and the Restrictions for Illyrian Dales Master Association, the specifications, architecture, design, appearance, elevation and location of (and landscaping around) all buildings of any type, including, but not limited to, walls, fences, swimming pools, antennae, sewers, drains, disposal systems, or other structures constructed, placed or permitted to remain in Utopia as well as the alteration, improvement, addition or change thereto.

Section 5. Insure Compliance with Master Land Use Plan. - - To insure compliance with the Master Land Use Plan under the Planned Unit Development Ordinance of Conch county, Florida, applicable to Utopia.

Section 6. Other. - - To provide, purchase, acquire, replace, improve, maintain and/or repair such buildings, structures, landscaping, paving and equipment, both real and personal, related to the health, safety, and social welfare of the members of the Association, as the Board of Directors in conjunction with the

Membership as required in the Declaration of Maintenance Covenants determines necessary, appropriate, and/or convenient.

Section 7. A Nonprofit Operation Solely for Member's Benefit. - - To operate without profit for the sole and exclusive benefit of its members.

Section 8. Subject to IDMA's Declaration and Enforcer of It in Utopia. - - To administer and manage portions of Utopia in accordance with the provisions of the Declaration of Maintenance Covenants of Utopia, the Declaration of Maintenance Covenants of Illyrian Dales Master Association, the Restrictive Covenant and the Restrictions for Illyrian Dales Master Association, and to enforce the provisions of such documents.

ARTICLE 3

General Powers

The general powers of the Association are as follows:

A) To accept and hold funds and title to the Common Areas solely and exclusively for the benefit of the members for purposes set forth in these Articles of Incorporation.

B) To promulgate and enforce rules, regulations, bylaws, covenants, restrictions and agreements to effectuate the purposes for which the Association is organized and in particular to enforce the provisions of the Declaration of Maintenance Covenants for Utopia and of the Declaration of Maintenance Covenants of Illyrian Dales Master Association and the Restrictions for Illyrian Dales Master Association.

C) To delegate power or powers where such is deemed in the interest of the Association.

D) To purchase, lease, hold, sell, mortgage or otherwise acquire or dispose/of, real or personal property; to enter into, make, perform or carry out contracts of every kind with any person, firm, corporation or association; to do any and all acts necessary or expedient for carrying on any and all of the activities and pursuing any and all of the objects and purposes set forth in the Articles of Incorporation and not forbidden by the laws of the State of Florida.

E) To contract for or coordinate private security, fire protection, insurance and other services but not to accept responsibility for the effectiveness of such private security, fire protection and other services.

F) To make and collect assessments to be levied against property to defray expenses, costs of effectuating the objects and purposes of the Association and losses of the properties owned by it, to create reasonable reserves for such expenditures, and to authorize its Board of Directors to enter into agreements with associations or other property owners' groups for the collection of such assessments.

G) To charge recipients for services rendered by the Association and the user for use of Association property where such is deemed appropriate.

H) To pay taxes and other charges, if any, on or against property owned or accepted by the Association.

I) To borrow money and, from time to time, to make, accept, endorse, execute and issue debentures, promissory notes or other obligations of the Association for monies borrowed or in payment for property acquired or for any of the other purposes of the Association and to secure the payment of such obligation by mortgage, pledge, or other instrument of trust, or by lien upon, assignment of or agreement in regard to all or any part of the property rights or privileges of the Association wherever situated.

J) To transfer to Illyrian Dales Master Association, Inc. such of its duties, powers and obligations as may be necessary or desirable.

K) To enforce, by legal means, any and all covenants, regulations, restrictions, agreements, assessments and laws applicable to Utopia.

L) In general, to have all powers conferred upon a corporation by the laws of the State of Florida, except as prohibited herein.

ARTICLE 4

Members

Section 1. Link between Lot Owners and UPOAI Members. - - The Members will consist of the Lot Owners in Utopia, the Property comprising Utopia being described in Exhibit A annexed to the Declaration of Maintenance Covenants. All such Lot Owners will be members of the Association. Membership in this Association will be related to, and may not be separated from, ownership of any Lot in Utopia. There will be one class of members in Utopia and it will include all owners of Lots in Utopia.

Section 2. SLAPP Lawsuits Barred. - - As a matter of public policy in Florida, SLAPP lawsuits — that is, a "Strategic Lawsuit Against Public Participation" — is forbidden because such actions are deemed inconsistent with the right of parcel owners to participate in the state's institutions of government. Therefore, the Florida legislature found and declared that prohibiting such lawsuits by governmental entities, business entities, and individuals against parcel owners who address matters concerning their homeowners' associations will preserve this fundamental state policy, preserve the constitutional rights of parcel owners, and assure the continuation of representative government in the State of Florida. A parcel owner sued in violation of this section has a right to an expeditious resolution of a claim that the suit is in violation of this section. A parcel owner may petition the court for an order dismissing the action or granting final judgment in favor of the parcel owner. The petitioner may file a motion for summary judgment, together with supplemental affidavits, seeking a determination that the lawsuit was brought in violation of this section. The entity initiating the lawsuit will thereafter file its response and any supplemental affidavits. As soon as practical, the court will set a hearing on the petitioner's motion, which will be held at the earliest possible time after the filing of response by the initiator of the lawsuit. The court may award the parcel owner being sued actual damages arising from the violation of this section. A court may treble the damages awarded to a prevailing parcel owner and will state the basis for the treble damages awarded in the judgment. The court will award the prevailing party reasonable attorney's fees and costs incurred in connection with a claim that the action was filed in violation of this section. A homeowners association may not expend association funds in prosecuting a SLAPP lawsuit.

ARTICLE 5

Voting

Section 1. Basic Vote. - - Subject to the two exceptions set forth in Section 2 below and any other restrictions and limitations hereinafter set forth, each Member will have one vote for each Lot which it owns. The vote of the Owners of a Lot owned by more than one natural person or by a corporation or other legal entity will be cast by the person named in a certificate signed by all of the owners of the lot, or, if appropriate, by the executive officers, partners or principals of the legal entity, and filed with the Secretary of the Association. The certificate will be valid until revoked and replaced by a subsequent certificate.

A residence owned by other than a single human — that is, either multiple human owners or a nonhuman entity, such as a corporation or trust — may not vote unless they or it filed a certificate designating an authorized voter with the Secretary of the Association. If the certificate is not filed with the Secretary of the Association at least three business days before a meeting in which the Owner might otherwise participate and/or vote, those Owners(s) are ineligible to vote and their vote will not be counted; furthermore, their existence will not count toward establishing a quorum at any meeting of members and the denominator of the fraction usually valued at 92 in determining the presence or absence of a quorum or the appropriate percentage majority of a vote must be decreased accordingly so that those ineligible voters are not counted as abstentions.

Section 2. Earned Votes. - - A Member may qualify for up to two (2) additional votes to cast as they see fit during their lifetimes at each annual, general, or special meeting of the members.

> A) A Lot owner may earn and cast an additional vote if they have resided in Utopia for at least ten (10) years prior to 2002 without incurring any fines or unsuccessfully suing the community.
>
> B) Similarly, a Lot owner may earn and cast an additional vote if they have successfully completed at least one full two-year term as a Director of the Utopia Property Owners Association, Inc. without being recalled or forced to resign.
>
> C) The award of any extra vote(s) must be confirmed by the current President of the Association or the head of Community Management Service firm retained by the Association at a Meeting of the Board or by a written petition to the Board signed by at least one-third of the members for it to take effect and the Minutes must note that award.

Section 3. Notice. - - Members who are owners of Lots in Utopia are entitled to have individual notice of all meetings of members delivered by mail or hand to their last known address in the Association's records.

> A) With an Owner's prior written consent, the Association may employ e-mail to transmit notices of Member meetings.
>
> B) The Association may also give supplemental notice via the cable TV channel used by Illyrian Dales for such purposes provided it meets the requirements set forth in Florida statute 720.
>
> C) As Utopia's only bulletin board is on a wall of the bathhouse which is rarely used and inconvenient for most members, notices of Board and/or members meetings posted on that bulletin board, at best, supplement rather than fully substitute for the notice delivery methods required above.

Section 4. Use of an Agent. - - Lot Owners may represent themselves in person or, at their sole discretion, by another person identified in writing as their agent, proxy or "attorney" on a form satisfying Florida's legal requirements for such a document and delivered to the Secretary of the Association at least three business days before it is to be used. Each Owner has an absolute and irrevocable right to appoint an agent or agents to conduct some or all of her or his affairs in Utopia by issuing a suitable proxy or power-of-attorney.

A) Only the Owner issuing such a proxy or power-of-attorney may call into question its abuse, nonuse or misuse, instructions or restrictions.

B) A proxy holder or attorney of record must act within the limits specified in the written proxy or power-of-attorney unless explicitly granted discretion to act or not act as s/he sees fit in their principal's interest. In either case, the designated agent cannot have greater freedom of action or inaction than the principal.

Section 5. Voting. - - A Member may vote in person or by using an absentee ballot or by taking appropriate measures to authorize an agent to cast her/his ballot(s).

Section 6. Ballots. - - All ballots will consist of two separable sections with a unique number identifying each ballot appearing on both sections of each ballot. One section of each ballot will record the Member's vote(s) for the candidates or position on the issue(s), The other section must be signed by the Member or their duly designated agent to validate the ballot and the fact that the Member did or did not vote in the election at hand.

Section 7. Vote Counting. - - Votes must be counted and tallied by employees of the Community Management Service firm retained by the Association under the visual scrutiny of two unrelated Members. The employees are assigned by the head of the Community Management Service firm retained by the Association. The members overseeing the vote count are appointed by the President with the advice and consent of the Board from those in attendance who are eligible to run for a Board seat but are neither Directors nor candidates for a Directorship at the time of the vote.

Section 8. Penalty for Not Voting. - - Members must vote in all elections and on all matters requiring a vote in Member's meetings. Members are to be notified annually by mail that failure to vote carries a fine unless they can provide a doctor's certificate showing that a sudden personal medical emergency in their immediate family prevented them from voting. Members who do not vote are to be warned once by mail immediately after their first failure to vote that they will be fined $10 if they do not vote at the next opportunity, $20 if they fail to vote at their second opportunity, $40 if they fail to vote at their third opportunity, $80 if they fail to vote at the fourth opportunity and $100 for each failure to vote thereafter.

Section 9. Funding Restrictions. - - The Association will obtain funds with which to operate by assessment of its members in accordance with provisions of the Declaration of Maintenance Covenants and Restrictions for Utopia, as supplemented by the provisions of the Bylaws of the Association relating thereto.

ARTICLE 6

Assessments

Section 1. General. - - Utopia POAI funds its activities with maintenance and special assessments of its Members. Maintenance assessments raise funds for routine activities — that is, ordinary and usually ongoing activities other than emergencies. Emergencies may be funded with special assessments if and only if there either are no reserves designated for that purpose or the established emergency reserve was exhausted. A special assessment cannot be used to start or replenish any reserve or increase the money in any reserve to a higher than previously authorized level or to fund a special project.

Section 2. Restrictions on Assessments. - -

A) Special assessments may only be used to partly or fully finance capital improvements if and only if all the procedures specified elsewhere for reviewing and approving capital improvements were followed exactly and all of the following requirements also are fulfilled exactly as specified.

B) No more than one (1) regular assessment may be levied in any calendar or fiscal year. No more than (1) special assessment may be levied in any calendar or fiscal year unless it becomes necessary to raise additional funds to deal with an emergency.

C) A separate membership meeting is required to review and approve any proposed special assessment. If the special assessment is intended to partly or entirely fund a special project or capital improvement, the membership meeting to review and approve it must be scheduled no sooner than 30 business days after the membership meeting required to review and approve the special project of capital improvement to allow time for the membership to obtain, read and understand the information which must accompany that notice.

D) A separate membership meeting is required to review and approve any proposed maintenance assessments which either individually or collectively total more than $1,000 per household per year.

E) No special assessment may be requested or levied:

1) if it commits the Board or the community to any unspecified or vaguely specified future expenditures or not fully described special projects;

2) for any item(s) in whole or part already in the annual budget; or

3) for any item(s) which are part of an ongoing or not fully described larger project.

F) Notice of the membership meeting addressing any special assessment must satisfy all of the following requirements.

1) It must be legibly typed, dated, in English, on Utopia stationery, and sent to all owners stating the date, time, and place of the meeting at least 30 business days prior to the meeting and signed by at least one officer of UPOAI's Board of Directors. The mailing must be attested to by a certificate signed by an officer of the Board and filed at the Association's office.
2) The notice must list and clearly and fully describe the specific purpose(s) to be funded by the special assessment and state the total amount of the special assessment as well as the amount per household. If more than one payment is allowed, then the notice must also state the amount per household per payment and any savings from paying the full amount per household.
3) The notice must state that the funds sought are expected to suffice based on realistic bids in hand and that any surplus will be refunded pro rata to the homeowners within 30 calendar days of completion of the project(s).
4) If the special assessment is insufficient to fully fund the proposed project(s), then the notice must describe all the other sources of funds which will in combination with the special assessment fully fund the proposed project(s) and provide all relevant details of those financial arrangements. In no event may a special assessment be levied unless the requisite funding arrangement is complete and approved by the membership.
5) If the special assessment involves funding more than one project, in whole or part, the notice must present all of the information called for above both in total and broken down by project.

G) For notification and operational purposes, projects may not be combined or lumped together if they logically or actually are unrelated or can be completed separately; conversely, projects which are related logically or factually in nature or over time may be not addressed piecemeal but must be described and funded together. [For example, projects to create different residential communities are separable and must be treated as such. Conversely, a project to build an individual house may not be decomposed into separate projects to buy land for the site, clear the land, obtain blueprints and permits, excavate for foundation, pour the foundation, install the floors and walls, install the roof trusses, finish the roof, put siding on the exterior walls, install the plumbing pipes and fixtures, run the electrical wiring, install the heating and air-conditioning system, etc.]

ARTICLE 7

Reserves

Section 1. General. - - It will be the policy of Utopia Property Owners Association, Inc. [UPOAI] to establish and maintain financial reserves for various purposes.

Section 2. Commingling. - - The funds of various reserves may be commingled in a common account if and only if accounted for separately.

Section 3. Diversion. - - Funds reserved for a particular purpose may not be diverted to another reserve or another purpose except to help pay for an extreme emergency when the funds in the emergency or general reserve have been exhausted.

Section 4. Funding of Reserves. - - All reserves must be funded by regular maintenance assessments, donations, and/or earned interest but never by a special assessment.

Section 5. Purposes. - - Other than a general reserve for unspecified emergency purposes, reserves may only be created for specifically and completely described infrastructure related purposes such as power washing and painting the exteriors of residences and community owned buildings, road repair / replacement, fixing or replacing all or part of the irrigation / sprinkler system or sewers or water pipes or the pool, and the like, including capital improvements. Routine activities such as tree removal, planting and/or pruning, flower planting and grass replacement are not infrastructure activities for these purposes.

No reserve may be created or used to hold idle balances simply "to make the community look good" or "rich" or enhance its "prestige."

Section 6. Trees and Reserves. - - Removal of trees downed by a hurricane or tornado and/or their replacement are a matter for the general emergency reserve to fund unless a separate reserve is created just for this purpose.

Section 7. Target Size and Time to Target of Reserves. - -

A) The average target size of the general or emergency reserve is 25% of Utopia's annual operating budget with an acceptable target range from a threshold of 20% to a maximum of 30%, rounded down to the nearest $5,000, and excluding accumulated earned interest.

> 1) The Board may fully spend this reserve to cope with an emergency.
>
> 2) If this reserve's total funds, excluding accumulated earned interest, exceeds 30% of UPOAI's annual budget, the excess funds must be returned proportionately to the homeowners who contributed to that fund. That refund must be completed within 60 calendar days after the end of that fiscal year unless intervening events require spending that surplus to resolve a new emergency.
>
> 3) If the emergency reserve falls below the 20% threshold as defined above as a result of an emergency and that same emergency or a later one requires spending more than the rest of that reserve's funds plus routine dues and collections over the next three months would not offset the difference, the Board must propose levying a special assessment to cover the necessary additional emergency spending and defer restoring the emergency reserve in whole or in part until three months after the emergency is over. Then the Board must increase monthly dues the level necessary to restore the emergency reserve's funds to the 20% threshold over the next three years under the

assumption that no emergency occurs in that future period provided however that any dues increase not exceed $22 per household per month.

4) The portion of an annual maintenance assessment to enrich the emergency reserve may not exceed $11 per household per month once that reserve's fund, excluding accumulated earned interest, exceeds the 20% threshold.

5) Homeowners may not be assessed for the emergency reserve after its funds, excluding accumulated earned interest, exceed 30% of the annual operating budget.

B) Any and all other existing reserves must have target size and timing rules similar to those for the emergency reserve explicitly associated with them by the Board within a year after these governing documents are recorded and those rules must appear in the Minutes. Any new reserves must have similar target size and timing rules established when they are created. In no case can those reserves collectively have either funds greater than that of the maximum size of the emergency reserve or larger or faster monthly replacement amounts than the emergency reserve.

ARTICLE 8

Board of Directors

Section 1. Board of Directors as the Association's Administrative Body. - - The affairs of the Association shall be administered by a Board of Directors consisting of not less than three (3) and not more than nine (9) Directors.

A) The Board may vary in size with an odd number of Directors within the above stated limits based on the availability of eligible candidates and their election unless and until the community authorizes a different number at the annual meeting or a special meeting of the members called for that purpose or the other Board members choose not to appoint qualified individuals to fill any vacancies created by a recall or resignation without precluding the establishment of a quorum based on the original size of that Board.

B) No Member may serve more than four (4) two-year terms as a Director or member of a Board committee and those terms must be non consecutive, that is, there must be at least a two (2) year gap between any term served by a given individual and her/his next term; an appointment to the Board to fill a vacancy counts as a full term if it lasts more than four (4) months.

C) The Directors preferably will be, but need not be, members of the Association, part- or full-time residents of Utopia or residents of the State of Florida.

D) The Board may only fill vacant positions with eligible persons starting with the individual who garnered the greatest number of votes in the prior election but failed to win a seat and working down the list of failed candidates. The Board may only appoint from outside the list of unsuccessful candidates from the immediately prior election if none of those individuals are now eligible, able or willing to serve.

Section 2. Staggered Terms. - - To preserve continuity, Directors will be elected at the annual meeting of Members to serve staggered two-year terms unless appointed by the other Directors to fill the remainder of a former Director's term where the latter died, resigned or was recalled. Approximately half of the Directors will be elected in even-numbered years. The remaining Directors will be elected at the next annual meeting.

Section 3. Recall. - - Directors may be recalled with or without cause being stated by the affirmative vote of a majority of the members eligible to vote and voting either at a special meeting called solely for that purpose or simply by a petition signed by such a majority of members and subject to the further provisions herein, the Bylaws and state laws, notably Florida statute 720.303 (10)(a - j). A recall at a meeting takes effect immediately but a recall by petition only takes effect after the Community Management Service firm retained by the Association has validated its signatures. Owners may appoint agents to act for them in these matters.

Section 4. Resignations. - -

A) A Director may resign at any time without stating a reason but must notify an officer of the Board in writing of that intention and the date when that resignation takes effect.

B) The notified officer must deliver the written resignation to the Board for action at its next regularly scheduled meeting.

C) The Board must acknowledge receipt of any resignation by noting it in the Minutes before it can take effect.

D) A Director's death is an automatic resignation in so far as the Board is concerned.

Section 5. Suspension. - -

A) A Director must be immediately suspended from Board service for a breach of fiduciary duty after previously being given one warning. The suspension becomes an automatic resignation and renders the Director in question permanently ineligible for future service on the Board and its committees unless s/he requests a hearing within 30 business days of the event at either a special meeting of the members called as soon as possible and solely for that purpose or as part of the next annual meeting of the members and obtains a majority vote of approval.

B) A breach of fiduciary duty includes, but is not limited to:

1) a lack of trustworthiness as evidenced by senility, persistent refusal to obtain objective information, relying on the opinions, hopes or whims of others instead of objective facts and/or not acting logically on those objective facts, lying by presenting false information or distorting or withholding relevant information, censoring information to the Board or the general membership, and/or making allegations which either are unsubstantiated or cannot be objectively and independently substantiated;

2) a lack of independence as evidenced by a visible and lasting commitment to a faction in the community rather than the long-term best interests of the majority of the members or frequent deferral to the opinions of others on or off the Board;

3) two or more incidents of quibbling over trivia, that is, pettifoggery;

4) two or more attempts to usurp or discredit the authority of the Board or any of its officers or committee chairmen;

5) two or more exhibitions of ignorance of the relevant laws and governing documents;

6) two or more misinterpretations of the relevant laws and/or governing documents;

7) two or more demonstrations of inability or unwillingness to obey the relevant laws and/or governing documents;

8) relying on or advocating such irrational or inappropriate arguments or sophistries as:

>[a] Other Boards allow/disallow XYZ or communities to do or not do XYZ so we can too;
>[b] Who does it hurt?;
>[c] We don't care about the rules, we just want to have fun;
>[d] We represent the majority of the community so the Board need not consult them even if the documents say we must;
>[e] We know what the majority of the community wants or will want so the Board need not consult them even if the documents say otherwise;
>[f] Only a few dollars are involved so the rules don't matter;
>[g] It's a simple matter so we can do this informally;
>[h] We've or others have done this before and not been called on it or penalized for it so we can do it again;

[I] The Board can do whatever it wants;

[j] As Directors we can do whatever we want; the rules don't apply to us in our public or personal lives; and

[k] The majority of the minority using the pool area should set the rules for pool area use and determine the amount of the community's funds to be spent on the pool area and on what those funds should be spent.

9) incurs a conflict of interest and/or the appearance thereof by putting personal preferences or financial advantage or the interests of her/his family, friends or business colleagues ahead of that of the majority of the community;

10) communicates or works so badly with other Directors and/or staff personnel that they prefer not to deal with her/him or is vicious or vengeful;

11) is persistently unable or unwilling to devote sufficient time and effort to carry out her/his Board responsibilities in a timely and adequate fashion; has to be prodded or reminded to complete assignments;

12) suggests or attempts to circumvent the notification and/or quorum requirements with "workshops," "briefings," "training sessions," "informal social affairs," "e-mail," "private phone calls or facsimiles," or

13) tolerates, promotes or encourages any of the above in others.

C) The presiding officer and all directors are primarily, but not solely, responsible for immediately and publicly notifying a peer of her/his breach of fiduciary duty. A Director's failure or refusal to immediately warn a peer of potential breach of fiduciary duty means that s/he too has breached her/his fiduciary duty.

D) Notice of breach fiduciary duty also may be given to the Board in writing if signed by:

1) the representative of the Community Management firm retained by the Association or anyone else advising the Board on parliamentary matters;

2) any three past Directors who successfully completed at least one term of office without being challenged for breach of their fiduciary duty or recalled;

3) a petition from at least one-third of the members; or

4) the attorney retained by the Board or any other attorney licensed to practice in the State of Florida and specializing in matters of governing homeowners associations.

Section 6. Board Meetings. - -

A) A meeting of the Board of Directors of the Utopia Property Owners Association, Inc. [UPOAI] occurs whenever a quorum of the Board gathers to conduct association business. A quorum is established by the presence of one Director more than one-half of all Directors.

B) All Board meetings must be open to all members except for meetings between the Board and its attorney with respect to proposed or pending litigation where the contents of the discussion would otherwise be governed by attorney-client privilege.

C) No Board business may be transacted at a Board meeting unless proper notice was given and a quorum established. Deliberating conducting Board business without proper notice and a quorum is a per se violation of the fiduciary duty of all Directors participating in it and renders null and void all motions and/or resolutions, orders, and decisions made by the Board at that session.

D) Members or their duly authorized agents have the right to attend all meetings of UPOAI's Board of Directors and to speak for at least three minutes on any matter placed on the agenda by petition of the voting interests.

1) The Association may adopt written reasonable rules expanding the right of members or their agents to speak and governing the frequency, duration, and other manner of member statements, provided those rules are consistent with this paragraph and may include a sign-up sheet for those wishing to address the Board.

2) Notwithstanding any other laws, the requirement that Board meetings and committee meetings be open to the members is inapplicable to the portion of meetings between the Board or a committee of the Board and the association's attorney held for the purpose of discussing personnel matters.

E) If 20 percent of the total eligible voting interests petition the Board to address an item of business, the Board will put the petitioned item on the agenda for its next regular Board meeting or at a special meeting of the Board, but not later than 60 calendar days after the receipt of the petition. The Board will give all Members notice of the meeting at which the petitioned item will be addresses in accordance with the 14-day notice requirement of Florida statute 720.303 (c)(2).

1) Each Member or duly designated her/his agent will have the right to speak for at least three [3] minutes on each matter placed on the agenda by petition, provided that they sign the sign-up sheet, if one is provided, or submits a written request to speak to the Secretary of the Board prior to the meeting.

2) Other than addressing the petitioned item(s) at the meeting, the Board is not obligated to take any other action requested by the petition.

F) Board meetings will operate according to the planned agenda accompanying the notice of the meeting unless after establishing a quorum a majority of the Board votes to alter the agenda's sequence and/or add items.

1) The agenda will have the following major items and must address them in the order listed below:

   [a] roll call of the Directors present in person or by speaker phone;

   [b] announcement that a quorum was or was not established;

   [c] read and approve or amend the Minutes of the prior meeting;

   [d] read aloud any correspondence received;
   [1] if a letter of resignation was received, this is the time to accept it

   [e] hear, discuss, and vote to accept or amend the reports of the Treasurer, then the standing committees, and then those of any ad hoc committee(s);

   [f] announce that the Board will discuss and vote on the items of old business either in the order mentioned on the agenda accompanying the meeting notice or as revised at the start of the meeting after hearing any relevant comments from attending Members or their duly authorized representatives and do so;

   [g] announce that the Board will discuss and vote on the items of new business either in the order mentioned on the agenda accompanying the meeting notice or as revised at the start of the meeting after hearing any relevant comments from attending Members or their duly authorized agents and do so;

   [h] open the floor for questions, comments and/or criticisms from Members or their duly authorized agents; and

   [l] adjourn.

2) Deviation from the procedure immediately above automatically invalidates all decisions and/or acts by the Board with respect to all items on the agenda and requires automatic suspension of the presiding officer for breach of her/his fiduciary duty.

G) The meeting notice and the accompanying agenda must explicitly state that a budget or assessment or proposed change will be discussed and provide all appropriate details. It also must list any non routine item to be brought up for discussion which might involve an expenditure of $1,000 or more.

H) Board meetings will operate in accordance with Robert's Rules of Order unless a majority of the Board votes to suspend those rules for part or all of a particular meeting.

Section 7. Receivership. - - In the event of a failure to fill sufficient vacancies on the Board of Directors to reestablish a quorum in accordance with the Bylaws, any Member may apply to the circuit court that has jurisdiction over Utopia POAI for the appointment of a receiver to manage the affairs of the association. At least 30 calendar days before applying to the court, the Member will mail to the Association, by certified or registered mail, and post, in a conspicuous place on the property of the community served by the association, a notice describing the intended action, giving the Association 30 calendar days to fill the vacancies. If during such time the Association fails to fill a sufficient number of vacancies to assemble a quorum, the Member may proceed with the petition. If a receiver is appointed, the homeowners' Association is responsible for the salary of the receiver, court costs, attorney's fees, and all other expenses of the receivership. The receiver has all the powers and duties of a duly constituted Board of Directors and will serve until the association fills a sufficient number of vacancies on the Board so that a quorum can be assembled.

Section 8. Minutes Required. - - Minutes of all meetings of the members of UPOAI and its Board of Directors must be maintained in written form or another form that can be converted into written form within a reasonable time.

A) Any Board committee(s) with the final authority to spend community funds and/or alter the established Architectural standards must give suitable notice of its meetings, keep its meetings open, and generate Minutes of its meetings which are turned over to the Secretary, but committees without such powers need not do so.

B) The vote or abstention from voting on each matter by each Director and/or committee member must be recorded in the Minutes for each Director or committee member present at the meeting of the Board or committee.

C) All Minutes of UPOAI are public records and so are available for any Member of the association or their duly appointed agent(s) to read without charge provided they have given reasonable notice, preferably but not necessarily in writing, to the association. Members also are entitled to copies of the Minutes provided reasonable written notice is given and may not be charged more than twice the going commercial per page rate within a ten-mile radius of the association office for such copies.

Section 9. Prohibitions. - - Under no circumstances may the Board of Directors of Utopia Property Owners Association, Inc.:

A) make a donation or contribution to a political campaign, religious group, or trade or professional association;

B) pay to join a trade or professional group or reimburse Directors for doing so;

C) contemplate, discuss, vote to pursue or participate in a legal action to seek an injunction or damages in response to apparent or actual defamation of Utopia, its Board or any of its Directors unless it has in hand a clear preponderance of objective evidence showing that the supposed defamatory act(s):

1) was done with malice aforethought rather than out of ignorance, frustration, or in the heat of the moment, and
2) caused at least $30,000 in damages.

ARTICLE 9

Officers

Section 1. Association Administered by Officers. -- The affairs of the Association will be administered by the officers of the Association which will be a President, a Vice President, a Secretary and a Treasurer, and such other officers as the Board may from time to time by resolution create with the advice and consent of the members by a supermajority of the eligible voting interests by the process described elsewhere in these governing documents.

A) No director may hold more than one office at the same time with two exceptions.

1) The posts of Secretary and Treasurer may be combined by resolution of the Board.

2) The offices of the President or Vice President, on the one hand, and either the Secretary or the Treasurer on the other hand may not be combined save in an emergency and then for no longer than 60 calendar days.

B) Officers will be elected for one (1) year terms in accordance with the procedure set forth in the Bylaws.

Section 2. Election of Officers. -- Officers are elected by the Directors from the currently serving directors. Officers serve at the pleasure of the Board and can be removed with immediate effect at any time, with or without cause being given, by a majority vote of the Directors.

Section 3. Fiduciary Standards. -- Officers are required to meet the highest fiduciary standards while serving so as to set an example for the other Directors and to assure the community of the Board's trustworthiness.

> A) As fiduciaries, officers must take active measures to avoid the appearance of any violation of the law or governing documents, especially in matters of actual or potential conflict of interest. Officers must fully and promptly disclose to the Board any potential or actual conflict of interest and must abstain from voting whenever they have a conflict of interest which might reach or exceed or reasonably be worth $50 or more.
>
> B) As fiduciaries, officers must take active measures to assure that the other Directors understand their fiduciary duties and honor that duty or give one warning and on the next violation suspend them for breach of fiduciary duty.

Section 4. Signatory Authority. - - Only officers may sign checks. They may not delegate this power to anyone else. Two officers must sign each check.

ARTICLE 10

Corporate Existence

The Association will have perpetual existence.

ARTICLE 11

Bylaws

The Board of Directors will adopt Bylaws consistent with these Articles.

ARTICLE 12

Amendment to Articles of Incorporation

These Articles of Incorporation may be altered, amended or repealed only by following the procedure for doing so set forth in the Declaration of Maintenance Covenants' Article 9 Section 8 and the detailed procedure set forth Article 4 Section 9.

ARTICLE 13

Indemnification

Section 1. Commitment to Indemnify. - - The association hereby commits to promptly indemnify any Director, officer or member of any committee appointed by the Board of Directors or President made a party to or threatened to be made a party to any threatened, pending or completed action, suit or proceeding whether civil, criminal, administrative, investigative unless one or more of the conditions stated below are violated. Any such indemnification will include the costs of: judgment, fines, reasonable attorneys' fees and expenses actually and necessarily incurred as a result of such action, suit or proceedings or any appeal thereof. To qualify for indemnification the party or parties in question must have:

A) acted in her/his capacity as a Director of Officer of the Association or member of a committee of the Association's Board of Directors, or as the agent of any other corporation, partnership, joint venture, trust or other enterprise which s/he served at the request of the Association;

B) in any civil matter(s) acted in good faith and diligently rather than negligently to establish a reasonable belief that such action was in the best interests of the Association and not a conflict of interest, or

C) in any criminal action(s) or proceeding(s) had acted diligently rather than negligently and in good faith to establish reasonable ground to believe that such action was lawful;

D) prevailed rather than settled or pleaded nolo contendere or its equivalent unless the remaining board members not party to such action unanimously finds that it was in the Association's best interests to do so.

E) been subject to an action by a party or parties other than the Association where the latter exercises its right, whether civil, criminal, administrative, or investigative, other than one by or in the right of the Association to procure a judgment in its favor, brought to impose a liability or penalty on such person for an act alleged to have been committed by such person in his capacity as Director or officer of the Association, or in his capacity as Director, officer, employee or agent of any other corporation, partnership, joint venture, trust or other enterprise which he served at the request of the Association.

F) not been adjudged guilty of negligence or misconduct in the performance of her/his duty to the Association unless and only to the extent that the court, administrative agency, or investigative body before which such action, suit or proceeding is held will determine on application that, despite the adjudication of liability but in view of all circumstances of the case, such person is fairly and reasonably entitled to indemnification for such expenses which such tribunal will deem proper.

Section 2. Association's Power to Indemnify. - - The foregoing rights of indemnification will not be deemed to in any way limit the powers of the Association to indemnify under applicable law.

ARTICLE 14

Conflict of Interest

Section 1. General. - - No contract or transaction between the Association and one or more of its Directors or officers, or between the Association and any other corporation, partnership, association or other organization in which one or more of its Directors or officers are Directors or officers, or have a financial interest, will be invalid, void or voidable solely for this reason, or solely because the Director or officer is present at or participates in the meeting of the Board or committee thereof which authorized the contract or transaction, or solely because his or their votes are counted for such a purpose so long as the Director's conflict of interest does not raise the value of the Lorenz-Gini Coefficient above the 0.2000 value stipulated in the Declaration. No Director or officer of the Association will incur liability by reason of the fact s/he is or may be interested in any such contract or transaction provided s/he also satisfies the requirements in the other section of this Article.

Section 2. Effect of a Conflict of Interest on a Quorum. - - Interested Directors may be counted in determining the presence of a quorum at a meeting of the Board of Directors or of a committee which authorized a contract or transaction.

ARTICLE 15

Dissolution of the Association

On dissolution of the Association, all of its assets remaining after provision for creditors and payment of all cost and expenses of such dissolution will be distributed in the following manner:

Section 1. Real Property. - - The Association's real property will be sold and the money received distributed equally among the Lot Owners after deducting the cost(s) of the sale.

Section 2. Personal Property. - - The remaining assets net of any associated legal or handling expenses will be distributed equally to the Lot Owners.

ARTICLE 16

Definitions

All terms used herein which are defined in the Declaration of Maintenance Covenants for Utopia will be used herein with the same meanings as defined in said Declaration.

BYLAWS OF UTOPIA POA, INC.

ARTICLE 1

Definitions

Section 1. Referral to Declaration. - - The terms used in these Bylaws will have the same meanings ascribed to them in the Declaration of Maintenance Covenants for Utopia Homes at Illyrian Dales.

Section 2. Subordination. - - These Bylaws will be and are subordinate to the provisions of this Association's Declaration of Maintenance Covenants and its Articles of Incorporation. In the event of a conflict between these Bylaws and either the Declaration of Maintenance Covenants or the Articles of Incorporation, the Declaration of Maintenance Covenants will govern both the Articles of Incorporation and these Bylaws. Similarly, the Articles of Incorporation will govern these Bylaws in the event of a conflict between the Articles of Incorporation and these Bylaws.

ARTICLE 2

Location of Principal Office

The principal office of this Association will be located in Conch County within a ten (10) mile radius of Utopia at such place as may be established by resolution of the Board of Directors.

ARTICLE 3

BOARD MEETINGS; NOTICE; PROXIES; ASSESSMENTS

Section 1. Meetings. -- Meetings will be scheduled on the third Monday of each month and at times and locations convenient for the majority of the Members of the Association. Meetings will only be held in premises which are accessible to the disabled, within a 10-mile radius of Utopia, adjacent to parking for at least 20 cars, quiet for recording purposes, air conditioned for members' health and comfort, have a speaker phone connection, have ready access to the Association's records, and which are neither likely to be interrupted by other activities nor likely to interfere with other activities.

Section 2. Meeting Notices. -- Notices of all Board must be mailed or hand delivered at least 14 business days prior to the meeting, except in the case of an emergency.

- A) Notices may be sent by facsimile, e-mail or other electronic means with the prior written consent of the Member(s) as long as they provide their working fax number or e-mail address.

- B) Any notice broadcast on closed circuit cable must appear at least four times every broadcast hour of each day for the same period as a written notice is required. Broadcast notices must contain the agenda and be broadcast in a manner and for sufficient continuous length of time so as to allow an average reader to observe the notice and read and understand the entire content of the notice and the agenda.

- C) Supplemental notices also may be posted on the bulletin board at the pool but are not sufficient notice in and of themselves.

- D) To be valid, the notice at the least must:
    1) be issued on Utopia stationery;
    2) be dated as of the day issued;

3) state the location, day and time of the meeting;
4) present the detailed agenda items in their planned order of discussion with all reasonably foreseeable or planned item of old and new business; and
5) be signed by an officer, preferably the Secretary or President.

Section 3. Assessment Notice. - - An assessment may not be discussed or voted on at a Board meeting or a Members meeting unless the notice of the meeting included a statement that assessments will be considered and provides the details called for elsewhere in these documents.

Section 4. Voting by Directors. - -

A) Directors must vote in person or via speaker phone at Board meetings. Directors may not have an agent represent or vote for them at a Board meeting. Directors may not vote at Board meetings by absentee ballot or secret ballot, except that secret ballots may be used in the election of officers. A Director may, however, have a duly authorized agent represent her/him at and cast her/his vote in Members meetings.

B) Agents or proxies may not be used to establish a quorum at a Board meeting or a meeting of a Board committee, but duly authorized agents may be used at meetings of Members to establish a quorum and to speak and vote for their principal(s).

C) Directors and officers must vote on each motion or resolution before the Board unless required to abstain so as to avoid the appearance or actuality of a conflict of interest. Those votes must be recorded in the Minutes.

D) Any Director who feels inadequately informed or uncertain about the merits of any change under consideration must vote against any proposed change to the status quo.

ARTICLE 4

Members

Section 1. Quorum; Amendments. - -

    A) The percentage of voting interests required to constitute a quorum at a meeting of the Members will be 30% of total eligible voting interests. Unless otherwise required elsewhere in these documents, decisions that require a vote of the members may be made by the concurrence of a simple majority of the voting interests present, in person or by absentee ballot or as represented by a duly authorized agent at a meeting at which a quorum has been established.

    B) Unless otherwise provided in these governing documents as originally recorded or permitted by Florida statute, an amendment may not materially and adversely alter the proportionate voting interest related to a parcel or increase the proportion or percentage by which a parcel shares the common expenses of the Association unless the record parcel owner and all record owners of liens on the parcels join in the execution of the amendment. For these purposes, a change in quorum requirements is not an alteration in voting interests.

Section 2. Annual Meeting. - - The Association must hold a meeting of its members annually for the transaction of any and all proper business at a time, date, and place stated in, or fixed in accordance with, these Bylaws. The annual election of Directors is required and must be held in conjunction with the annual meeting. The notice for the annual meeting must include a detailed agenda showing the order of business and the specific items to be addressed including all reasonably foreseeable or planned components of old and new business and must be signed by an Association officer.

    A) The annual meeting of the members will be held on the third Monday of January each year or as soon as practical thereafter but no later than the third Monday in March at the principal office of this Association, and at such time or at such other place in Conch County, Florida, as may be established by the Board of Directors subject to the conditions set forth elsewhere in these Bylaws.

B) A written notice of such meeting will be served by the Secretary on each Member personally, or by mail addressed to each Member at his address as it appears on this Association's records. If all of the Members are present, or if the absent Members have previously waived notice in writing, the notice requirements will be dispensed with.

C) The voting privileges of a Member will be suspended if s/he is delinquent on any assessment or any installment.

D) Eligible candidates are encouraged to campaign for a Directorship during reasonable hours by introducing themselves to other residents, expressing their interest in serving on the Board, citing their credentials and/or reasons for seeking a Directorship. Candidates may make "cold calls" and may leave flyers or newsletters with residents who are willing to accept them. Candidates may not broadcast flyers or newsletters or post them or signs in the community or spend more than $200 campaigning no matter the source of those campaign funds.

Section 3. Special Meetings. -- Special meetings of the members may be called at any time by the President or a majority of the Directors. Special meetings of the members must be held as soon as practical if called for by the President, a majority of the Board or by signed petition from 10 percent of the total eligible voting interests of the Association and no later than sixty (60) calendar days from the call date or the receipt of a petition whichever is earlier. If an emergency disrupts the schedule, the meeting may be rescheduled to a date no more than another thirty (30) calendar days beyond the original date. Business conducted at a special meeting is limited to the purposes described in the notice of the meeting. Notice of such meeting stating the purpose for which it is called will be served by the Secretary on each Member personally, or by mail addressed to each Member at his address as it appears on this Association's records. If all of the Members are present, or if the absent Members have waived notice in writing, the notice requirements will be dispensed with.

Section 4. Notice of Meetings. - - The Association will give all parcel owners and members actual notice of all membership meetings, which will be mailed, delivered, or electronically transmitted to the members not less than 14 business days prior to the meeting. Evidence of compliance with this 14-day notice will be made by an affidavit executed by the person providing the notice and filed on execution among the official records of the Association.

Section 5. Right to Speak. - - Members and parcel owners have the right to attend all Board and membership meetings and to speak at any Board or membership meeting with reference to all items opened for discussion or included on the agenda. A member and a parcel owner or their duly authorized agents have the right to speak for at least three (3) minutes on any item, provided that they submit a written request to do so to the Secretary of presiding officer prior to the meeting. Utopia POAI may adopt written reasonable rules governing the frequency, duration, and other manner of member and parcel owner statements, which rules must be consistent with this subsection.

Section 6. Adjournment. - - Adjournment of an annual or special or meeting to a different date, time, or place than originally stated in the notice must be announced at that meeting before an adjournment can take place, or written notice must be given of the new date, time or place. Any business that might have been transacted on the original date of the meeting may be transacted at the meeting rescheduled in the adjournment. If a new record date for the adjourned meeting is or must be fixed under Florida statute 617.0707, notice of the adjourned meeting must be given to all persons entitled to vote and are Members as of the new record date but were not Members as of the previous record date. A meeting may be adjourned because of inclement weather, an inability to establish a quorum, an emergency disrupting the meeting, insufficient time to complete the agenda or deal wisely with items added to the agenda, or to stop disruptive behavior.

Section 7. Proxy Voting by Members. -- Members have the right to appoint a duly authorized agent to cast their vote — that is, a vote by their proxy or "attorney" — in person or via an absentee ballot or via a regular ballot if the agent attends the meeting in person.

A) To be valid, the document authorizing an agent, attorney or proxy to act for the Member — that is, a principal — must state the date, time, and place of the meeting for which it was given, must be signed by the Member or authorized person issuing it, and state any directions or restrictions on the agent's freedom of action or the agent will be presumed to have authority to act with full discretion.

B) Only Lot owners eligible to vote or their attorneys can authorize an agent to act for them.

C) A proxy or similar delegation of authority to an agent is effective only for the specified meeting for which it was originally given, as the meeting may be lawfully adjourned and reconvened from time to time, and automatically expires 90-business days after the date of the meeting for which it was originally given unless it clearly gives the agent authority for a longer period.

D) Any delegation of authority to an agent is revocable at any time at the pleasure of the person who executes or issues it provided the revocation is in writing and copies are sent to the agent and the Association office or the presiding officer at a meeting where the agent would otherwise act for her/his principal.

E) If and only if the delegation of authority or proxy expressly so provides or allows, a duly authorized agent may appoint, in writing, a substitute to act in her/his place.

F) Written delegations of authority to an agent must be filed with the Association office at least three business days before taking effect.

G) Only the person who delegated authority to an agent may object to her/his agent's interpretation, scope of authority, use, nonuse or abuse of that authority and then must be able to provide convincing objective proof of the merit(s) of her/ his objection or remain silent.

H) Any duly authorized agent must be assumed to have full discretion to act for her/his principal unless the form authorizing her/him to act clearly states otherwise or provides explicit instructions or decision rules limiting such discretionary power.

I) Duly authorized agents must be: counted in place of their principal to establish a quorum, taken into account when determining the outcome of a vote, and allowed to speak for their principals in membership meetings, Board meetings and Board committees.

Section 8. Elections. - - Elections must be governed by the procedures set forth in various places above in these documents or immediately below as to notice, nominations, eligibility to vote, vote counting, recording and so forth.

Section 9. Nominations for Directors. - - Nominations for Directors may be obtained in three ways.

A) A standing Nominating Committee must be appointed to solicit and screen nominations, including self-nominations, from eligible candidates according to procedures established for it below.

B) Alternatively, eligible individuals may run for a seat on the Board by either announcing their intent to run from the floor at the appropriate time before the vote at the annual meeting or delivering a petition signed by at least 30% of the eligible voters to the Secretary before the start of the annual meeting.

1) People running from the floor or by petition are the only acceptable write-in names on the ballots.

2) People running from the floor or by petition must be eligible candidates according to the criteria set forth elsewhere in these documents or votes for them do not count.

Section 10. Eligibility for Board Service. - - Only qualified individuals are eligible to serve as an Officer, Director or member of a Board committee. Individual members may be temporarily or permanently ineligible to run for a Directorship or to serve on the Board or any of its committees for a variety of reasons including, but not limited to, the following:

A) Any one who has been recalled or forced to resign for breach of fiduciary duty is permanently ineligible to serve on the Board or any of its committees.

B) Term limits as set forth above in these documents also may render an individual temporarily or permanently ineligible to run for a Directorship or to serve on the Board or any of its committees.

C) Anyone convicted of a felony in the United States of America is ineligible for Board service unless they can show that their right to vote has been restored.

D) Anyone whose past behavior indicates to a majority of the community that they are unable or unwilling to consistently act as a trustworthy fiduciary for the best long-term interests of the majority of the community is permanently ineligible to serve on the Board or any of its committees.

E) Anyone who instigated or participated in an unsuccessful lawsuit or administrative proceeding against Utopia is ineligible to serve on the Board or any of its committees.

F) Anyone who has unsuccessfully sought a Directorship for three or more consecutive years is ineligible for the next three years.

G) Within two years of having these governing documents recorded, the Board must establish a training program for those on the Board and/or its committees as well as seeking to fill such positions in the future Directors. Once that program is established, only those who successfully complete it are eligible to serve on the Board or any of its committee, provided they also satisfy all other eligibility requirements.

Section 11. Recording. - - Any parcel owner, Member or resident may tape record or videotape meetings of the Board of Directors and meetings of the members. The Board of Directors of the Association may adopt reasonable rules governing the taping of meetings of the Board and the Members.

Section 12. Record Date. - - The Board of Directors may fix a time in the future for determining which members are entitled to notice of and vote at any regular or special meeting of the members. Such record date shall not be less than ten (10) business days nor more than forty (40) business days prior to the date set for a meeting of the members. Only persons who have closed on their purchase of a residence in Utopia and are members on this Association's records as of three business days prior to the meeting shall be entitled to vote at any regular or special meeting.

ARTICLE 5

Directors

Section 1. Board of Director's Authority and Qualifications for Directorships. - - The affairs and business of this Association shall be managed, and its corporate powers exercised, by a Board of Directors as outlined in the Articles of Incorporation. The majority of Directors shall be homeowners, the legally wedded spouse of a homeowner or the legally authorized agent of the homeowner if that homeowner is a non-human entity such as a corporation, trust, or partnership. Directors need not be primarily or permanently or exclusively residents of the State of Florida. Directors must be eligible to serve according to eligibility standards set forth elsewhere in these governing documents. Nonresident owners and part-time residents are entitled to Directorships in rough proportion to the share of the community's residences they represent based on rounding that share down to the nearest 10% and provided that rounded down number does not exceed 50% of the total Directorships. Only in certain extraordinary circumstances described elsewhere in these documents, may a Director not be a homeowner, the legally wedded spouse of a homeowner or the duly authorized agent of a homeowner.

Section 2. Board Meetings. - - A regular meeting of the Board of Directors shall be held immediately following the members annual meeting, and at such time as the Board of Directors may determine. Special meetings of the Board of Directors may be called by the President at any time, and shall be called in a reasonable time by the President or the Secretary upon the written request of a majority of the Directors or in response to a petition signed by at least 10% of the members. Directors' meetings may only be held within a 10-mile radius of the Association's primary office and are subject to conditions set forth elsewhere in these governing documents.

Section 3. Service of Meeting Notices. - - Notice of meetings, other than the regular annual meeting, shall be given by service upon each Director in person, or by mailing to him at his last known post office address, at least 14 business days (including the day of mailing) prior to the date therein designated for such meeting. The notice shall specify the time, day and place of such meeting, and provide the planned agenda showing the order of business and the planned and reasonably foreseeable items of business to be brought before the meeting. At any meeting at which every member of the Board of Directors shall be present or if the absent Directors consent in writing, any routine business may be transacted even if the notice requirements were not met. However, unless proper notice as described elsewhere in these governing documents is given, the Board may not entertain or address any matters which also require the advice and consent of the Members, such as a proposed change in operating procedure under the governing documents, amendment of the governing documents, the structure or operations of the Board or its committees, policy changes, assessments, capital improvements, reserves, and so forth.

Section 4. Members as Observers; Right to Speak. - - Meetings of the Board are open to all members and residents as observers with a limited right to speak and no right to vote. Unless a Member serves as a Director or has been specifically invited by the Directors to participate in a meeting, the Member is only entitled to observe any meeting of the Board unless s/he invokes her/his right to address the Board for no more than three minutes on an issue before the Board according to the rules set forth elsewhere in these governing documents. The Board must hear any and all member's comments on or questions about any particular issue before the Board immediately before otherwise addressing that issue and must respond fully to those questions before finishing its discussion.

Section 5. Voting by Directors. - - Each Director shall have one vote and the act of a majority of the Directors present in person or via speaker phone at a meeting at which a quorum is present at the time of the vote shall be the act of the Board of Directors.

Section 6. Filling Board Vacancies. - - The Board may, but need not, fill any vacancy arising between annual elections provided there are enough remaining Directors to constitute a quorum.

> A) If the Board chooses to fill a vacancy, it must first offer the position to the individual who garnered the highest number of votes without winning a Board seat at the immediately prior annual election. If that individual is unwilling or unable to accept, then the Board must approach the next such person and so on until either filling the opening or exhausting the list of such individuals.
>
> B) If and only if no immediately prior but unelected candidate(s) is available, eligible and willing to serve, the Board may attempt to fill the vacancy by appointing any other eligible Member willing to serve or it may call a special election.

C) If still unable to fill the vacancy but able to achieve a quorum based on its original size, the Board may instead: operate as a smaller entity until the next annual election, pick an eligible Member at random to fill the vacancy or ask the presidents or vice presidents of the nearest homeowners associations to serve for a fee not to exceed $100 per outsider per meeting attended.

Section 7. Waiver of Notice. -- Whenever by statute, the provisions of the Articles of Incorporation or these Bylaws, the members of the Board of Directors are authorized to take any action after notice, such notice may be waived, in writing, before or within 10 business days after the holding of the meeting by the person or persons entitled to such notice.

Section 8. Quorum. -- At any meeting of the Board of Directors, a majority of the Board shall constitute a quorum for the transaction of business, but in the event of a quorum not being present, a lesser number may adjourn the meeting for not more than fifteen days.

Section 9. Executive Committee. -- The Board of Directors may, by resolution, designate by name and/or function two or more of their number to constitute an Executive Committee, who, to the extent provided in such resolution, shall have and may exercise the powers of the Board of Directors in an emergency and then for no longer than sixty (60) consecutive calendar days. Any resolution establishing an executive committee must be passed with sixty (60) business days of a Board taking office or it is invalid.

Section 10. Exercise of Board's Powers and Duties. -- All of the powers and duties of the Association, including those under the Declaration of Maintenance Covenants, the Articles of Incorporation and any other Documents, shall be exercised by the Board unless otherwise specifically delegated by a Board resolution, which is noted in the Minutes, to one of the Board's committees or the members. Such powers and duties of the Board shall be exercised in accordance with the provisions of these governing Documents and shall include but not be limited to the following:

A) Making, establishing, amending and enforcing reasonable rules and regulations governing the "Common Areas" subject to the restrictions and procedures set forth elsewhere in these governing documents.

B) Making, levying, collecting and enforcing assessments against members to provide funds to pay the "Association's Expenses". Such assessments shall be collected by the Association by payments made directly to the Association by the members in the manner set forth in the Documents.

C) Maintaining, managing, administering, operating, repairing and replacing the improvements and personal property of the Association on, to or within the Common Areas.

D) Constructing and reconstructing or removing improvements located in the Common Areas over which the Association has jurisdiction in the event of casualty or other loss thereto and making further authorized improvements therein subject to the restrictions and procedures set forth elsewhere in these governing documents.

E) Enforcing by legal means the provisions of the Documents as set forth elsewhere in these governing documents.

F) Retaining independent contractors and professional personnel and entering into and terminating service, supply and management agreements and contracts to provide for the administration, management, operation, repair and maintenance of the portions of Utopia over which the Association has jurisdiction, including the delegation to third parties of powers of the Board with respect thereto.

G) Hiring and retaining employees and/or contractors as are necessary to administer and carry out the services required for the proper administration of the Association and paying all of the salaries therefor.

H) Paying costs of all power, water, sewer and other utility services rendered to the portions of Utopia over which the Association has jurisdiction and which are not billed to individual "Owner".

I) Paying taxes and assessments which are or may become liens against any property located on the portions of Utopia over which the Association has jurisdiction and assessing the same against the Owners' "Lots".

J) Purchasing and carrying insurance for the protection of Owners and of the Association from and against any casualties and liability therefor with respect to the portions of Utopia over which the Association has jurisdiction in accordance with the Documents.

K) Maintaining and repairing the Lots including the water sprinkler system, grass cutting, shrub trimming, etc. through its duly authorized agents, servants and/or employees or by hiring an independent contractor(s) to perform said services upon a regular and continuous basis and billing the cost of all such expenses to the Owners as part of the Association Expenses.

Section 11. Nepotism. - - A spouse, sibling, parent, child, or other relative of a Board member or a member of a Board committee may serve on the Board or any standing or ad hoc committee of the Board if otherwise qualified to do so.

ARTICLE 6

Officers

Section 1. List. - - This Association shall have a President, a Vice President, a Secretary, a Treasurer. The creation or formation of additional officer positions may not be proposed by the Board and may only be enacted in strict accordance with the process for reviewing and approving or rejection proposed changes set forth elsewhere in these governing documents.

A) No officer may hold more than one office at the same time except in two cases.

   1) the offices of Secretary and Treasurer may be combined if the Board consists of five or less Directors.
   2) in an emergency the available Directors may function as an executive committee consisting of at least a presiding officer and an acting Secretary-Treasurer but that state of affairs cannot continue for more than sixty (60) consecutive calendar days.

Section 2. Election. - - All officers of this Association shall be elected annually from the Directors by the Board of Directors at its meeting held immediately after the annual meeting of the members or as soon thereafter as is convenient to the newly installed Board of Directors but not later than the next scheduled Board meeting.

A) The Board must reelect its officers if it fills a vacancy arising from a recall, voluntary or compulsory resignation, or demise of a Director.

B) The officers hold office at the pleasure of the Board of Directors and so can be removed from that office, but not their Directorship, at any time by a simple majority vote of the Directors without having to state, discuss or debate their reasons.

C) The Board may elect such other officers and appoint such other agents and employees as it shall deem necessary who shall have such authority and shall perform such duties as the Board shall prescribe from time to time according to the rules and procedures set forth elsewhere in these governing documents.

Section 3. Officer's Duties and Powers. - - The duties and powers of the Officers of this Association shall be as follows:

A) The President shall be the chief executive officer of this Association; have general and active management of the business and affairs of this Association subject to the directions of the Board of Directors; and preside at all meetings of the members and Board of Directors.

1) By virtue of her/his office, the President is an ex officio member of all committees of the Board except the Nominating Committee. [Ex officio means that by virtue of the inherent authority of the office the President serves as a full-member, but not the chair, of all committees, except the Nominating Committee, with the right to observe, speak and vote.]

2) The chairs of all Board appointed committees, except the Nominating Committee, report to the President or, in the absence of the President to the Vice President; the Nominating Committee reports to the Board as a whole.

3) The President is responsible for:

[a] conducting all Board meetings according to the announced or properly revised agenda;

[b] seeing that those meetings follow the rules and procedures set forth in these governing documents;

[c] assuring that those meetings are conducted in an orderly, collegial, decorous and respectful fashion;

[d] assuring that each Director honors their fiduciary duty during those meetings; and

[e] dealing with the Association attorney if s/he first obtained a two-thirds vote of approval from the Board to do so for this specific matter at hand. All other Directors must obtain permission from the President before bringing a legal matter to the Board for permission to contact the attorney save that in the absence of the President the Vice President assumes this responsibility.

B) Only one Board member may serve on any given committee except in an ex officio capacity and only an outgoing Board member may serve on the Nominating Committee and that must be by appointment of the Board.

C) The Vice President shall perform all of the duties of the President in the latter's absence and such other duties as may be assigned by the Board of Directors or President. The Vice President has the same ex officio responsibilities as the President but may not serve on a committee or in a particular committee meeting when the President does so.

D) The Secretary shall see that the Community Management firm retained by the Association: has custody of, and maintains, all of this Association's records except the financial records; records in a book the names and addresses of all members; records the minutes of all meetings of the members and Board of Directors; sends out all notices of meetings; and performs such other duties as may be assigned by the Board of Directors or President.

> 1) The Secretary is personally responsible for seeing that the recordings of meeting Minutes are properly transcribed and that any obvious typographic errors are corrected before the next Board meeting and promptly brings any other questionable items to the attention of the officer who will preside at the next meeting of the Board.
>
> 2) The Secretary also is responsible for seeing that each Director has a copy of the transcribed and edited Minutes at least one full calendar week before the next scheduled Board meeting.

E) The Treasurer shall see that the Community Management Service firm retained by the Association has custody of all of this Association's checkbooks; financial records; keeps full and accurate accounts of receipts and disbursements and renders an account thereof at the annual meetings of members and whenever else required by the Board of Directors or President.

1) The Treasurer also is responsible for

   [a] seeing the Association's funds are in the care of reputable financial institutions;

   [b] causing an appropriate annual compilation, review or audit of this Association's books at the completion of each fiscal year by this Association's accountant and presenting the results thereof at the next regularly scheduled Board meeting; and

   [c] performing such other duties as may be assigned by the Board of Directors or the President.

2) The Treasurer must be covered by a fidelity bond, at Board expense, to give to this Association security for the faithful discharge of his duties; no one may serve as Treasurer unless so bonded.

3) The Treasurer must be able to balance a checkbook and explain the basic implications of Association's financial data in ordinary English but need not have any formal accounting/financial training or expertise.

F) No Board officer, Director or committee member may accept, solicit, donate, refer to another or promise another pay, gifts, finder's fees, or any other form of compensation from suppliers or Members for or in relation to their Board services. This restriction also applies to pay, gifts, finder's fee, or any other form of compensation given to a family member, friend or business colleague of a Board officer, Director or committee member in relation to Board services. Violation of this restriction is automatic grounds for suspension of the Director or committee member in question until an appeal hearing either clears them or declares them immediately and permanently ineligible for Board service.

Section 4. Delegation of Officer's Duties. - - In the case of the absence of any Officer of the Association or for any reason that the Board of Directors may deem sufficient, the Board may, except as specifically otherwise provided elsewhere in these governing documents, delegate the powers or duties of such Officers to any other officer or Director for an interim period not to exceed sixty (60) calendar days. Any officer unable to perform her/his duties after that sixty (60) calendar day period has lapsed must resign her/his position as an officer and as a Director.

ARTICLE 7

Committees

Section 1. Standing Committees. - - The only standing or permanent committees of this Association shall be: the Grounds Maintenance Committee; the Architectural Control Committee; and the Nominating Committee.

- A) Each standing committee shall consist of at least one but not more than three eligible persons aside from any ex officio member.

- B) The chair of each standing committee is nominated by the President and appointed with the advice and consent of the Board within thirty (30) calendar days of the annual meeting and serves until s/he resigns or is removed.

    1) The chair of each standing committee is responsible for informing the Board in writing of the identities of the other member(s) of her/his committee within 30 calendar days of being appointed.

    2) Each chair of a standing committee also is responsible for supervising and training the other members of her/his committee and assigning committee work to them.

    3) The chair also has the authority to remove any other member of her/his committee without consulting with the Board or having to publicly state a reason for doing so.

- C) No standing or ad hoc committee may have subcommittees.

D) No standing committee(s), ad hoc committee(s) or informal group(s) may be assigned or allowed to assume and/or act with any of the powers delegated to any other standing or ad hoc committee. If an overlap in the powers or duties of two committees arises, the chairs of those committees must resolve it and report their solution to the Board. If the chairs cannot agree on a solution to an overlap within 30 calendar days, the Board must address and resolve the issue at its next meeting with preference given to the recommendation from a standing committee over any ad hoc committee's recommendation.

E) It shall be the duty of each standing committee to receive complaints from members on any matter involving this Association's functions, duties and activities within its field of responsibility. It shall dispose of such complaints as it deems appropriate or refer them to such other committee, Director or Officer of this Association which is further concerned with the matter presented.

F) All members of a standing committee serve as fiduciaries and may be forced to resign for not doing so under the same procedures as set forth elsewhere in these documents for Directors.

G) No member of a standing committee may serve on any other standing or ad hoc committee except temporarily in an emergency.

H) No standing or ad hoc committee may have authority to commit the Association to a contract, make a final decision to spend Association funds, or actually spend Association funds in any amount whatsoever or alter the community's Architectural standards. Breach of this restriction requires the standing committee in question to give 14-business days written notice of all of its meetings with the agenda to all Members of the community, keep all of its meetings open to all Members of the community, and keep Minutes of all of its meetings and promptly and publicly give those Minutes to the Board as part of Association's official records.

Section 2. Powers and Duties of the Grounds Maintenance Control Committee. - - The Grounds Maintenance Control Committee shall advise the Board of Directors on all matters pertaining to the maintenance, repair or improvement of common ground and structures thereon as described and defined elsewhere in these governing documents and shall perform or see to the performance of such other related functions as the Board, in its discretion, determines.

> A) This committee has the power to issue warnings for violations of the relevant portions of the governing documents and to insist that the Board assemble an ad hoc committee to decide if a finable violation has occurred.

Section 3. Architectural Control Committee. -- The Architectural Control Committee [ACC] has the duties and functions described elsewhere in these governing documents and shall perform and see to the performance of such other functions as the Board determines in conformity with the rules for making changes set forth elsewhere in these governing documents.

> A) The Architectural Control Committee [ACC] shall apply and enforce reasonable, explicit and objective standards; it may not rely on subjective criteria such as personal aesthetics, tastes or preferences or the opinion of any group no matter how large. The ACC may recommend additional standard, revisions to existing standards, and/or termination of existing standards to the Board of Directors provided it does so in writing; any such recommendation is subject to the review and approval process for changes set forth elsewhere in these governing documents. Among the standards the ACC will apply and enforce are:
>> 1) The Architectural Control Committee shall see that resident's carports conform to Conch county's Property Maintenance Code Ordinances and Uniform Development Code as follows:
>>> [a] Items may be stored in a carport if and only if they are not hazardous or noxious, do not prevent a car from being parked in the carport and the stored objects are in good working order.

[b] Items may be stored freestanding, hanging from or leaning against the walls, or hanging from the ceiling.

[c] The ACC may not establish or enforce color, design, size, quality, quantity or other standards for things stored in a carport beyond those in Conch county's rules.

[d] Propane tanks and propane burning barbecues are not considered a fire hazard as long as they are in good working condition, are not rusty and are less than five (5) years old.

[e] Nothing may be stored in a carport if it produces: objectionable noise at the property lines between dusk and eight p.m., or electrical or magnetic interference, physical vibration, heat, glare, smoke, dust, odor or other nuisance outside the carport.

[f] A nonworking appliance being repaired or disassembled for parts may be stored in the carport for no more than sixty (60) consecutive calendar days.

[g] A carport may be used to conduct a hobby such as handicrafts.

[h] A carport may not be used to conduct a commercial enterprise but it may be used to store tools and parts for work done elsewhere by the homeowner.

[i] Carports were not designed to be and may not be enclosed, permanently or temporarily, whether with doors, screens or other materials unless being used as a temporary shelter for people during an emergency.

[j] Besides cars, items which may be and commonly are stored in carports include: bicycles, folding chairs, garbage containers, gardening tools and

supplies, golf carts and/or clubs, hurricane shutters, portable barbecue grills and fuel for such grills, workbenches and tools, spare roof tiles, and work tools such as ladders, shovels, and wheelbarrows.

[k] Carport walls and ceilings shall be painted the same color and shade as the exterior of the residence according to a sample maintained by the ACC.

[l] Carport floors may be left unpainted to show the original cement or painted in one of three approved colors and shades to match the exterior walls of the four-plex residential building containing it or the coral roof tiles of that building or the same black color and shade as the driveways.

[m] In order to maintain uniform architectural standards, including appearance, as much as possible, residents must store as much of their goods as possible in the closet of the carport rather than openly and keep everything stored openly as neat as possible, especially when not in use.

[n] Residents either in the same building as a carport they believe in violation of the above regulations or in line of sight of that carport from the front window(s) or door of their residence may petition the ACC for relief. The petition must be in writing and signed by those objectors. The objection must be investigated promptly by the ACC and if found valid tell the homeowner to cease and desist. If the homeowner refuses, the ACC must report the violation to the civil authorities. However, if the ACC recommends, the Board may grant a brief exemption for a homeowner to have her/his residence repaired or in cases of extreme emergency.

2) The Architectural Control Committee shall see that all driveways have the same black color and shade as the macadam used to pave the driveways. Driveways may not be resurfaced with "pavers" instead of macadam or painted any other color. Any deviation from this subsection is to corrected immediately at the owner's expense and, if not, the ACC must insist that the Board immediately have the violation corrected and record a lien against the residence in question for the cost of effecting those repairs so as to avoid creating a vested interest on the part of the homeowner contrary to the community's architectural standards.
3) The Architectural Control Committee shall see that homeowners maintain and repair their tile roofs with the same design/style, color and shade of tile as the original roofs at the homeowner's expense.

   [a] Before having such work done, the homeowner must complete and file with the ACC an appropriate written application and await written approval from the ACC and IDMA's ACC. Any firm hired by the homeowner must either submit documented proof that it is suitable licensed, insured and experienced to the ACC or be on record at the Association office as having done so.

   [b] No work may be started until the ACC verifies that all required permissions and permits have been obtained and properly filed and posted.

   [c] Temporary repairs of an emergency nature may be made without seeking or waiting for ACC's permission in order to prevent damage to the homeowner's residence or an adjoining residence.

4) The ACC shall see that exterior walls, window frames, doors, gutters and down spouts conform to the original design and colors of the community.

5) The ACC shall see that a homeowner's patio

[a] roof and/or screen supports are not installed at any point to a height greater than one foot below the tile roof, but the ACC has no control over the patio roof material or color;

[b} is, if enclosed, finished to conform to the rest of the residence's exterior stucco and color but has no control over the style, size, number design or color of any door from the patio to the outside, screening or screen supports, or windows;

[c] may, if it has a door to the outside, have an outside stoop or flat area adjacent to that door and which if new extends no more than five feet from the foundation and no more than two feet beyond each side of that door but the ACC has no power over the design or choice of materials used to construct that stoop; and

[d] is properly approved for enclosure, if the homeowner chooses to do so by using a suitable contractor but the ACC has no power over the amount of the patio area to be enclosed or the design or style of the enclosure save as stated in items a - c immediately above.

6) The ACC shall see that all infrastructure conforms to the original design standards or subsequent authorized changes thereto.

B) Any deviation from this subsection's standards must be brought to the owner's attention immediately with a written demand that it be corrected at the owner's expense within sixty (60) calendar days or as soon as possible thereafter if the necessary part(s), material(s) or labor are not immediately available.

1) If a violation is not corrected promptly corrected or if the Owner refuses to do so, the ACC must insist at the next regular Board meeting that the Board have it

corrected at the Board's expense and record a lien against the residence in question for the cost of effecting those repairs so as to avoid creating a vested interest on the part of the homeowner contrary to the community's architectural standards.

2) A vested right or interest in favor of a homeowner is deemed to have been created if the Board allows a breach of Architectural standards to persist for a calendar year after its initial occurrence. After a year, that violation ceases and the homeowner thereafter has a vested right or interest contrary to the intent of the governing documents and established Architectural standards.

> [a] Once established, a vested right or interest not only exists for the current homeowner and all subsequent purchasers of that property but, to avoid discrimination, for all other Utopia homeowners and all subsequent buyers of their residences.
>
> [b] Once a vested right or interest is established, the Board must make an immediate good faith effort to correct or negate a vested right or interest by asking, but not compelling, the homeowner to waive that right or interest in exchange for the Board restoring the situation to the status quo ante at the Board's expense either as soon as possible or prior to any subsequent sale or transfer of title to that property.

C) A party aggrieved by a decision of the Architectural Control Committee shall have the right to make a written request to the Board of Directors, within thirty business days of the decision, that it be reviewed by an independent ad hoc committee appointed by the Board. That ad hoc committee shall consist of three individuals who are not Board members, relatives, friends or business colleagues of any serving Board member and not relatives, friends or business colleagues of the aggrieved party. That ad hoc committee may consist of individuals who are neither members of the Utopia POAI nor resident in Utopia. That ad hoc committee shall hear the evidence of both parties and make its recommendation to the Board based on the facts presented to it and the rules of the governing documents. The determination of the Board, upon reviewing the Committee's decision, shall in all events be final, provided it does not overrule the ad hoc committee's recommendation without clearly stating a sound and logically supported reason for doing so.

D) The Board of Directors is responsible for promptly resolving any conflict(s) between its committees arising from an overlap of their assigned duties if the chairs of those committees are unable or unwilling to do so to their mutual satisfaction in the long-term interests of the majority of the community.

Section 4. Composition, Powers and Duties of the Nominating Committee. - - The Nominating Committee shall be chaired and staffed by a member who is neither a current Director nor intends to seek a Directorship in the next election; a second member of the committee must be a current Director whose term expires with the upcoming election or does not intend to run for reelection in the upcoming election. The third member of the committee must be a person who does not intend to run for a Directorship in the upcoming election.

A) The first duty of the Nominating Committee is to obtain a list from the Secretary of those community members eligible to serve as a Director according to the rules and guidelines set forth elsewhere in these governing Documents and a statement as to the number of Directors seats to be filled at the next election.

B) The committee's second duty is to meet and draft a letter to the Members soliciting nominations with a specific deadline, a clear statement of the information required and the format to be used.

1) That letter must be dated, issued on Utopia stationery and signed by the chair of the committee. It must be issued no later than the end of business of the first business day in September and include a deadline of for receipt of nominations no later than the first business day in October.

2) The letter must clearly state that nominations may be self-nominations, that without exception all nominations will be ignored if late or incomplete or if the nominee is either ineligible to serve under the rules in the governing documents or unwilling to do so, and that the committee reserves the right to publish the information obtained as received or in a standard format. The letter must also transmit a one- or two-page nomination form.

3) The committee also is responsible for obtaining a written affirmation from and signed by each nominee that they are interested in and willing to serve on the Board as a fiduciary, understand the implications of that term and, if elected, know and will abide by the relevant laws and rules and procedures in the governing documents.

4) The completed one- or two-page nomination form enclosed in the letter must be legible and in English. Whoever submits it to the Nominating Committee must identify the nominee by name and address in Utopia. It also must contain clear and accurate statements of the nominee's relevant credentials, including but not limited to prior board experience, length of ownership / residence in Utopia, and reason(s) why the nominee is interested in serving on the Board.

C) The committee's third duty is to meet to review and evaluate the nominations of those eligible as well as able and willing to serve.

1) If more nominees pass this initial screen than there are openings to fill, then the nominees must be rated and

a slate of recommended candidates prepared, rather than a mere list of candidates with their recapped credentials, for submission to the membership by inclusion in the election packet.

2) The document prepared by the committee containing the slate or list of candidates should identify the candidates in alphabetic order by last name, use a standard format to summarize each candidate's credentials based on information extracted from the nomination forms, and, if a slate is required, put an asterisk after the name of the candidates forming the recommended slate.

3) The committee may solicit additional information from or about the nominees by interviewing them or from personal knowledge of them and use that information in evaluating the candidates.

D) The committee's fourth duty is to deliver its list or slate to the Community Management firm before the end of business on the first business day of the deadline explained below, hand a safety copy of that document to the Secretary of the Association and to retain a copy until the election packet is mailed. The deadline for delivering the Nominating Committee's list or slate to the Community Management Association firm is 45 business days before the date of the forthcoming annual meeting and election.

E) The committee's fifth and final duty is to remain independent of any and all Board influence during its operations and to prevent any meddling with the recommendations it submits to the Community Management firm or the other documents the latter is to prepare and enclose in the election packet.

Section 5. Ad Hoc Committees. - - The Board of Directors may, from time to time, appoint such other ad hoc committees as it desires provided that they do not have the potential to or actually do interfere with, duplicate, impinge on or usurp the duties of any standing committee(s).

A) Ad hoc committees are temporary by nature and are intended to deal with a specific issue and then expire. No ad hoc committee may be appointed for more than one year or allowed to continue the same duties under different name or have subcommittees.

B) An ad hoc committee may only present recommendations to the Board or the membership; it may not spend Association funds without prior written authorization and only within the limits of its written charter.

C) It shall be the duty of each ad hoc committee to receive complaints from Members on any matter involving this Association's functions, duties and activities within its field of responsibility. It shall dispose of such complaints as it deems appropriate or refer them to such other committee, Director or Officer of this Association which is further concerned with the matter presented.

D) All Members of an ad hoc committee serve as fiduciaries and may be forced to resign for not doing so under the same procedures as set forth elsewhere in these documents for Directors and standing committees.

E) No member of an ad hoc committee may serve on any other standing or ad hoc committee except temporarily in an emergency.

F) The Board may appoint ad hoc committees to facilitate preparation of a proposed budget, provide training to qualify residents for future Board service, screen applications to buy or lease a residence in Utopia, and so forth. An ad hoc committee for strategic or long-range is unnecessary as these governing documents constitute an ongoing strategic plan and provide ways and means to develop, enact and perform appropriately, by amendment, in response to future changes in legal, economic, social or technological conditions.

G) The Board may not authorize or fund a Social Committee or a Hospitality Committee. This in no way bars interested Members from forming and operating either or both such committees independently of the Board save that the Board reserves the right to make and enforce any rules it deems necessary regarding the use of common ground by such committees in addition to the long-standing rule that no Social Committee may use the pool area for an affair where food or drink are consumed unless that affair: was previously authorized by the Board at a Board meeting, is open to all residents and their guests, is not intended as a commercial fund raising event, and that the Social Committee removes all garbage from the pool area as soon as the affair ends.

H) No ad hoc committee may have authority to commit the Association to a contract, make a final decision to spend Association funds, or actually spend Association funds in any amount whatsoever or temporarily waive or alter the Architectural standards of the community . Breach of this restriction requires the ad hoc committee in question to give 14 business days written notice of all of its meetings with the agenda to all Members of the community, keep all of its meetings open to all Members of the community, and keep Minutes of all of its meetings and promptly and publicly give those Minutes to the Board as part of Association's official records.

ARTICLE 8

Budgets and Financial Reporting

Section 1. Budgets. - - The Association shall prepare or cause to be prepared an annual budget. The budget must reflect the estimated revenues and expenses for that fiscal year and the estimated surplus or deficit as of the end of the current year as well as the estimated year-end values of each existing or planned reserve.

A) The estimates used to prepare the budget must be based on objective data and realistic assumptions which must be identified and completely specified in an appendix to that document.

B) The budget must set out separately all fees or charges for recreational amenities, whether owned by the Association or another person or entity.

C) The Board must notify the Members that a preliminary Budget is being prepared and that they will have 30 business days to inspect it at the Association office and prepare comments or questions about it before it will be considered for approval at a Board meeting.

D) Within a reasonable period of time after the Board approves the annual Budget for the coming fiscal year but no longer than sixty (60) calendar days thereafter, the Association shall provide each Member with a copy of the annual budget at no charge or a written notice that a copy of the annual budget is available on request at no charge and state in that notice where or how to obtain the copy.

Section 2. Financial Reporting. -- The Association shall prepare an annual financial report within sixty (60) days after the close of its fiscal year. Within a reasonable period of time after the Board approves the financial report for the prior fiscal year but no longer than sixty (60) calendar days thereafter, the Association shall provide each Member with a copy of the financial report at no charge or a written notice that a copy of the annual budget is available on request at no charge and state in that notice where or how to obtain the copy. Financial reports shall be prepared as follows:

A) The Association must prepare or cause its financial reports to be prepared in accordance with the Generally Accepted Accounting Principles. The financial statements shall be based on the Association's annual revenues, as follows:

1) if the Association's total revenues are at least $200,000 but not more than $400,000, then the Association shall prepare or cause to be prepared reviewed financial statements.
2) If the Association's total revenues exceed $400,000, then the Association shall prepare or cause to be prepared audited financial statements.

B) If 20 percent of the parcel owners petition the Board for a level of financial reporting higher or lower than that required here, the Association shall duly notice and hold a meeting of members within 30 business days of receipt of the petition for the purpose of voting on raising or lowering the level of reporting for that fiscal year. On approval of a majority of the total eligible voting interests of the parcel owners, the Association shall prepare or cause to be prepared financial reports at the authorized level of reporting in lieu of the level otherwise required by statute.

ARTICLE 9

Official Records

Section 1. Documents to be Retained. - - The Association shall retain for at least seven (7) years within the Association's office or at a nearby location under its control the originals of each of the following items, when applicable, which constitute its official records.

A) Copies of any bids, contracts, plans, specifications, permits, and warranties related to improvements constructed on the common areas or other property that the Association is required to maintain, repair or replace.

B) A copy of the governing documents and any recorded amendments thereto. The governing documents include the Summary Disclosure Statement, the Declaration of Maintenance Covenants, the Articles of Incorporation, and the Bylaws, the current rules of the Association and the standards applied by the standing committees.

C) The Minutes of all meetings of the Board of Directors, committees of the Board which are required to keep Minutes, and Members as well as any letters or reports to or from these entities.

D) A current roster of all members and their local and out-of-area mailing addresses, telephone / facsimile numbers, and, if they have one, their electronic or e-mail address for the purposes of sending notices to the members.

E) The Association's insurance policies or a copy thereof.

F) A current copy of all contracts to which the Association is a party, including without limitation, any management agreement, lease, or other contract under which the Association has any obligation or responsibility. Bids received by the Association for work to be performed also are official records and must be retained as such for a period of not less than one (1) year or until the work bid on is completed whichever is longer.

G) The financial and accounting records of the Association, kept according to good accounting practices. The accounting and financial records must include:

1) Accurate, itemized, and detailed records of all receipts and expenditures.

2) A current account and a periodic statement of the account for each Member, designating the name and current local address of each Member who is obligated to pay assessments, the due date and amount of each assessment or other charge against the Member, the date and amount of each payment on the account, and the balance due.

3) All tax returns, financial statements, and financial reports of the Association.

4) Any other records that identify, measure, record, or communicate financial information.

H) All other written records of the Association not specifically included in the foregoing which are related to the Association's operation.

Section 2. Access to the Association's Records. -- The books, records and papers of this Association shall at all times, during reasonable business hours, be subject to inspection by any Member without charge. Any Member may request copies of any of these documents with reasonable advance notice, preferably in writing, and at a charge of no more than twice the going commercial rate within a ten (10) mile radius and to have the requested documents available within ten (10) business days from time the Association receives her/his request.

A) The failure of the Association to provide access to the records within ten (10) business days after receipt of a written request creates a rebuttable presumption that the Association willfully failed to comply unless an obvious emergency delayed or prevented it from complying or if the records requested are not legally available to Members.

B) A Member who is denied access to official records is entitled to the actual damages or minimum damages for the Association's willful failure to comply with her/his request. The minimum damages are to be $50 per calendar day up to ten (10) days with the calculation to begin on the 11th business day after receipt of the written request.

C) The Association may adopt reasonable written rules governing the frequency, time, location, notice, records to be inspected, and manner of inspections, but may not impose a requirement that a parcel owner demonstrate any proper purpose for the inspection, state any reason for the inspection, or limit a parcel owner's right to inspect records to less than one 8-hour business day per month.

D) Certain Association Records are not publicly available, even to Members. Notwithstanding the other provisions of this Article, the following records shall not be accessible to Members or parcel owners:

> 1) Any record protected by lawyer-client privilege as described in Florida statute 90.502 and any record protected by the work-product privilege, including, but not limited to, any record prepared by the Association at the attorney's express direction, which reflects a mental impression, conclusion, litigation strategy, or legal theory of the attorney or the Association and was prepared exclusively for civil or criminal litigation or for adversarial administrative proceedings or which was prepared in anticipation of imminent civil or criminal

litigation or imminent adversarial administrative proceedings until the conclusion of the litigation or adversarial administrative proceedings,
2) Information obtained by the Association in connection with the approval of the lease, sale, or other transfer of a parcel.
3) Disciplinary, health, insurance, and personnel records of the Association's employees.
4) Medical records of parcel owners or community residents.

ARTICLE 10

Seal

This Association's seal shall be in circular form and have the name of the corporation inscribed thereon, and may be a facsimile engraved, printed or an impression seal.

ARTICLE 11

Amendments

Section 1. Sources of Amendment. - - These Bylaws may be altered, amended or repealed only by following the procedure for doing so set forth in the Declaration of Maintenance Covenants' Article 9 Section 8 and the detailed procedure set forth in Article 4 Section 9.

Section 2. Notice of Proposed Amendment. - - The Secretary will give each Member written notice of the Special Meeting, stating the date, time and place thereof, and enclosing a copy of the proposed amendment(s). The notice will be mailed not less than three (3) nor more than thirty (30) business days before the date set for the Special Meeting. If mailed, the notice will be deemed to have been properly given when deposited in the United States mail addressed to the Member at his post office address as it appears on the records of Utopia POA, Inc. with postage thereon prepaid.

A) Any Member may give a signed waiver of notice to be filed in the records of Utopia POA, Inc., which will be valid whether delivered before or after the holding of the meeting.

Section 3. Approval of Proposed Amendment. - - Any proposed amendment(s) must be approved by an affirmative vote of a supermajority described below of the votes eligible Members could cast in order for it to become effective.

A) For the first five years after these documents are recorded that supermajority will be 82%; thereafter the requisite supermajority will decrease in steps of 5% for each subsequent five-year interval after recording until it falls to 67%; thereafter the required supermajority will remain at two-thirds (2/3).

B) Each Lot Owner will be entitled to vote in person, by absentee ballot or have a duly authorized agent vote for them.

Section 4. Certification of Amendment(s). - - After approval, the amendment(s) will be transcribed into the Minutes by the Secretary and then certified by the President and Secretary as having been duly adopted, and the original or an executed copy of such certified amendment(s) will be recorded in the Public Records of Conch county, Utopia, within ten (10) business days from the date on which it or they were approved. The amendment(s) will specifically refer to the numerical recording data uniquely identifying this Utopia Declaration. Thereafter, a copy of the amendment(s) in the form in which the same were placed of record by the officers will be delivered to all of the Members of Utopia POA, Inc., but delivery of a copy thereof will not be a condition precedent to the effectiveness of such amendment(s). However, no amendment will reduce the maintenance provisions of this instrument below that required by the Conch county Subdivision and Platting Regulation Ordinance in effect as of September 30, 1978.

Section 5. Amendments and Mortgagees. - - Any amendment to these Bylaws which might affect the lien, security or value of security of any institutional first mortgagee, or the salability of a first mortgage on the secondary market, require(s) the written joinder and approval of at least two-thirds (2/3) of all institutions holding a first mortgage on real property of or in Utopia.

ARTICLE 12

Prior Resolutions and/or Motions

Section 1. Continuity of Board Motions and/or Resolutions. - - Boards of Directors of Utopia's Property Owner's Association, Inc. have, from time to time and for good and sufficient reason after due consideration of the matters in question, passed various resolutions and/or motions governing various aspects of the Board operations as well as Members behavior. Those motions and resolutions remain in effect until amended or revoked by statute, case law or the process for reviewing and approving such changes set forth elsewhere in these governing documents.

Section 2. Motions and/or Resolutions in Effect. - - Resolutions and/or motions still in effect include the following categories and items within those categories:

- A) Landscaping / Plants
    - 1) No fruit trees will be planted. [December 17, 1984]
    - 2) No bougainvillea flowers or vines allowed. [March 16, 1996]
- B) Late charges: There will be a late charge of $10.00 for any payment not paid by the 15th of the month [September 1982]
- C) Maintenance and/or repair
    - 1) The roofs of residences belong to the individual owners and it's their responsibility to maintain and/or repair them. [February 8, 1985]

2) Maintenance, repairs, and cleaning of gutters and down spouts are the homeowner's responsibility; and any beds and planting washed out due to excess water from gutters and down spouts are also the homeowner's responsibility. [May 18, 1987 and June 3, 1987]

D) Parking rules
   1) Parking is limited to one side of the street. [January 21, 1985]

   2) No parking on either side of the entrance to Utopia [November 16, 1987]

   3) Parking on Utopia Drive is prohibited except for social and business visitors. O and overnight parking banned unless written permission is obtained from the Board or the Security Office [February 28, 1994]

   4) $25.00 fines for parking violations [May 19, 1996]

E) Other: The Board of Directors will operate according to Robert's Rules of Order; and an officer must sign all correspodence. [February 17, 2004]

INDEX*

A

Absence 106, 147-149
Abstain 125, 133
Abstention 123
Access 55, 63, 78, 88, 95, 102, 132, 165, 166
Adjourn 121, 143
Agent 12, 21, 23, 36, 68, 78, 79, 81, 86, 88, 108, 126, 127, 133, 134, 137, 138, 140, 141
Amenity 7, 11, 92
Arrears 31
Articles of incorporation 14, 15, 61-63, 70
Association 5, 8, 9, 11-13, 15, 18, 28, 41, 42, 45, 55, 70, 91, 103-105, 120, 122, 123, 126
Attorney 1, 28, 42, 47, 49, 51, 54, 56, 58, 59, 108, 119, 120, 137, 166
Attorney-client privilege 79, 80, 119
Attorney fees 57, 65-67, 79
  incurring 65
Attorney's Fees 48
Authority 4, 29, 43, 69, 72, 102, 117, 137, 138, 146, 147, 150, 151, 162
  delegation of 137
Authorized agent vote 168

B

Bathhouse 3, 17, 18, 34, 93-96, 107
Benefits 4, 22, 27, 30, 31, 39, 53, 55, 79, 103
Bids xiii, 41, 111, 164, 165
  competitive 41, 42
Board 10, 23, 28, 42, 55, 117, 169
  affairs 20
  appointed committees 147
  approves 163
  bulletin 88, 107, 132
  business 119
  committee 14, 21, 24, 97, 115, 123, 133, 138, 139, 145
    members 24
    service 24
  constituted 122
  of Directors 2, 4-6, 14, 20, 40, 114, 119, 122, 123, 125, 126, 140-143, 146, 148, 149, 152, 157, 158
  of Director's Authority 140
  election 88
  expense 149
  influence 160
  installed 146
  meetings 43, 55, 97, 119, 120, 122, 133, 138, 147, 148, 162, 163
Board Meetings 82, 119, 132, 141
Board
  meetings
    regular 120, 156
    scheduled 146, 148, 149
    special 23
  member 114, 127, 145, 148, 157
  outgoing 148
Board Motions 169
Board
  officer 149
  operations 169
  prior 20
  reserves 161
  resolution 143
  responsibilities 102, 118
  seat 109, 142
  service 25, 116, 139, 149, 161
Board Vacancies 142

171

Board votes   120, 122
Board's
  committees   143
  expense   157
Board's policy   17
Board's Powers   143
Board's trustworthiness   125
Bonus   89
Budget   5, 35, 80, 122, 161-163
Budgets   5, 162
Bulletin board   88, 107, 132
Bylaws   1, 6, 8, 11, 15, 29, 42, 61-63, 70, 103, 109, 124, 125, 131, 134, 135
  authority   43
  of UTOPIA POA   131

C

Cancellation   41
CAP   48-50
Carport   97, 152-154
Certificate   33, 51, 67, 68, 86, 91, 106, 109, 111
Certification   37, 63, 85, 97, 168
Committee   21, 24, 28, 35-37, 43, 44, 46, 57, 120, 121, 123, 126, 138-140, 143, 145-152, 157-162
Common
  areas   2, 3, 7-9, 14, 17, 18, 24, 28, 30, 34, 38, 45, 76, 77, 102, 103, 144
  exclusive   2
  subject   144
  interest community   13
Common-interest community   13-15, 66, 68, 76, 77
Common Structural Elements   13, 17, 30
Compensation   40, 88-90, 149
Compliance   14, 27, 34, 42, 56, 58, 59, 64, 72, 77, 88, 136
Conch county   14, 17, 18, 96, 102, 152, 153
Conch County   5, 11, 42, 60, 131, 135
Conflict of interest   85, 87, 88, 125, 126, 128, 133
Construction   30, 40, 62, 89, 90, 97
Contract   6, 40-43, 80, 81, 89, 104, 128, 151, 162, 165
Contracts   40-43, 78-80, 89, 103, 104, 128, 144, 151, 162, 164, 165
Copy   18, 23, 41, 54, 60, 62, 68, 75, 78, 82, 148, 160, 163-165, 167, 168
Cost   3, 15, 17, 22, 32, 35, 38, 39, 46, 54, 57, 63, 77, 78, 94, 128, 145
Cost-benefit analysis   22, 35
Court   5, 6, 28, 34, 51, 54-56, 58-60, 64-67, 69, 78, 79, 83-85, 90, 105, 106, 122, 127
  order   60, 64, 65, 79, 90
Covenants   2, 3, 7, 9, 10, 34, 41, 43, 47, 59, 60, 91, 103, 105
  declarations of   8, 9, 53

D

Damages   4, 17, 20, 46, 50, 90, 106, 123, 124, 155, 166
  minimum   166
  risk of   20
DBPR   9
Declaration   2, 7, 14, 47, 52, 53, 60, 61, 69, 76, 77, 89, 91, 103, 128, 129
  of maintenance   126, 167
  of Maintenance Covenants   1, 2, 6, 7, 15, 29, 69,

103, 105, 109, 129, 131, 164
  of Illyrian Dales Master Association 102, 103
Declarations 9, 11, 15, 44, 64, 71
  of Maintenance Covenants 61-63, 70
Department 9, 18, 54-56
  of Labor's Bureau of Labor Statistics 48, 53
  mediators 55
Directors 9, 10, 24, 27, 28, 39, 44, 57, 88, 118, 124, 179
Director's authority 66
Directors, board of 20, 27
Director's
  conflict 128
  death 116
Directors, elected 87
Director's
  failure 118
  fiduciary duty 24
Directors
  offending 24
  recall 78
  recalled 82, 83, 85
  reimburse 123
  replacement 84
  seats 158
Disclosure 1, 41, 79, 97
Door 154, 156
Driveways 3, 38, 45, 154, 155
Dues 13, 31, 38, 39, 77, 113, 114
Duty 9, 24, 25, 66, 72, 97, 116, 118, 119, 122, 125, 127, 139, 147, 151, 158-161
Dwelling 1-5, 11, 13-19, 30-34, 39, 40, 47, 50, 62, 96, 97
  unit 4, 14, 16, 17, 19, 30-33, 39, 40, 47, 97

E
Election 51, 54, 55, 72, 76, 77, 86-88, 108, 114, 115, 124, 133, 134, 142, 143, 158, 160
Eligibility 21, 87, 138-141
Emergency 14, 20, 21, 42, 50, 53, 56, 58, 59, 61, 74, 76, 95, 109, 110, 112-114, 135, 136, 153-155
Employee 28, 80, 91, 127
Encroachment 16, 30
Encumber 37
Enforce 3, 26, 34, 41, 43, 59, 66-68, 103, 105, 152, 153, 162
Equipment 12, 41, 42, 48, 79, 97, 102
Equity 27, 59, 91
Expenditures, total 48, 49
Expenses 3, 18, 19, 34, 37, 41, 54, 55, 62, 80, 91, 92, 122, 126-128, 145, 155, 156, 162
  anticipated 5
  personal 22

F
Failure 27, 29, 31, 33, 55, 59, 81, 82, 109, 122, 166
Fairness xv, 64, 66
Fees 16, 28, 47, 49, 51, 54-56, 58, 59, 77, 89, 106, 122, 126, 143, 149, 163
  flat 89
FHLMC 34
Fiduciaries 9, 10, 88, 125, 151, 159, 161
  of members 44
Fiduciary duty 9, 24, 25, 97, 116, 118, 119, 122, 125, 139, 147
Fine 28, 92, 109

173

Fines 1, 27-29, 31, 51, 90, 92, 93, 96, 107, 126, 170
Foreclosure 29, 39, 44, 52, 56, 64, 65, 89, 91
  sale 64, 66
Foundation 19, 112, 156
Functions 2, 43, 88, 96, 143, 146, 152

G
Good faith 58, 72, 87, 88, 126, 127, 157
Governing documents 1, 10-12, 14-16, 24-27, 43, 44, 55-58, 61-63, 65-73, 75-77, 79-81, 85-91, 140-142, 144-147, 152
  alleged violations of 81
  attached 5
  revised 49
Gratuity 88
Guest 28, 46, 91
Guideline 19
Gutters 3, 155, 170

H
Hearing 24, 28, 45, 57, 106, 116, 121, 149
Homeowner 1, 15, 35, 56-59, 63-68, 71, 73-79, 81-91, 140, 141, 153-157, 170

I
IDMA 1, 2, 7, 8, 19, 26, 37, 43, 44, 62, 63, 103, 155
Illyrian Dales 1-3, 5, 7-9, 11, 14, 26, 27, 30, 43, 44, 54, 102-104, 107, 131
Improvement 15, 48, 50, 102, 110, 152
Incentive 89
Incorporation 1, 6, 8, 11, 14, 15, 26, 29, 61-63, 70, 103, 104, 126, 143
Indemnification 126, 127
Influence 88, 160

Infrastructure 20, 21, 112, 156
Inspection 35, 78, 92, 165, 166
Insurance 19, 38-40, 44, 48, 52, 62, 95, 104, 145, 165, 167
Interpretation 26, 43, 138

J
Judgment 4, 12, 24, 32, 51, 52, 60, 106, 126, 127

L
Landscaping 3, 46, 69, 89, 90, 102, 169
Lawns 38, 45
Laws 5, 6, 10, 27, 34, 52, 56, 57, 59, 64, 71-73, 75, 77, 81, 86-91, 104, 105
  applicable 58, 64, 66, 67, 127
  relevant 10, 43, 117, 159
Lawyer 89
Lessee 31, 32
Lessees 1, 31, 32, 46
Licenses 31, 62, 96
Lien xiv, 4, 7, 8, 12, 28, 34, 44, 47, 51, 52, 59, 61, 64, 90, 91, 104, 134
Limitation 16, 27, 38, 54, 91, 106, 165
List 40, 79, 111, 115, 122, 142, 145, 158, 160
Litigation 45, 59, 66, 79, 80, 119, 167
Lot xvi, 11, 14, 15, 18, 19, 29, 30, 38, 39, 46, 47, 50, 60, 97, 105-108, 128, 129, 137, 168
  owner 29, 39, 50, 107, 168

174

M

Maintenance 1-3, 5-8, 11-13, 19, 29-31, 38, 39, 45-48, 50, 51, 61-63, 102, 103, 109, 110, 131, 152, 167-170
Majority 4, 10, 22-26, 36, 37, 45, 58, 70, 75, 82, 84, 101, 115-118, 134, 135, 139-143
Management 15, 16, 40, 42, 43, 48, 70, 107, 108, 115, 119, 144, 146, 148, 160
Managers 39, 42, 87-91
Material 31, 156
Mediation 54-58, 80
Meeting 21-25, 36, 37, 48-50, 57, 74-76, 78-88, 97, 98, 106, 107, 110, 111, 114-116, 119-123, 132-138, 140-143, 148-151
Member 11, 12, 21, 24, 26-29, 45, 54, 60, 95, 96, 106-109, 122, 123, 135-137, 139-143, 147-151, 157, 158, 165-168
Minutes 25, 26, 78, 80, 81, 85, 93, 107, 114, 120, 121, 123, 142, 143, 148, 151, 162, 164
Mortgagee 38-40, 52, 61, 169
Motion 26, 106, 133

N

Notice 16, 32, 33, 36, 107, 110, 118, 132, 135, 141, 167
 of meetings 136, 148

O

Obligations 4, 13, 15, 32, 33, 38, 39, 102, 104, 165
Office 24, 72, 80, 85, 87, 91, 119, 124, 143, 146, 147
Officer 10, 16, 21, 24, 25, 27, 28, 35, 87-89, 97, 98, 111, 126-128, 133, 134, 136, 137, 145, 146, 148-151
Officers 10, 16, 20, 21, 24, 27, 28, 35, 81, 82, 87-91, 111, 116, 117, 124-128, 133, 145, 146, 150, 151
Ombudsman 49, 57, 78, 79, 84
Option 31, 39

P

Parcel 4, 7, 8, 11, 12, 14, 17, 18, 28, 29, 51, 52, 55, 63, 91, 105, 106, 134, 136, 164, 166, 167
Parking 132, 170
Patio 19, 93, 156
Payment 32, 40, 41, 52, 64, 104, 111, 128, 144, 165, 169
Permit 62, 65
Pet 91, 92
Petition 21, 25, 27, 34, 54, 76, 81, 82, 84, 85, 105, 107, 115, 119, 120, 122, 138, 139, 154
Petitioner 54, 55, 106
Pettifoggery 98, 117
Plan 2, 11, 14, 17, 31, 46, 56, 58, 65, 102, 161
Policy 17, 40, 44, 52, 78, 105, 112, 142
 public 78, 105
Pool 3, 17, 93-95, 102, 112, 132
Power washing 11, 112
 periodic 3
Powers 21, 26, 34, 43, 44, 47, 69, 70, 72, 103-

105, 122, 123, 143-146, 150-152, 156
corporate   140
delegate   103
discretionary   88, 138
implied   69
Precedence   6, 20, 26
Price   xi, 51
Principal office   84, 85, 131, 134
  location of   131
Priority   20, 39, 101
Privilege   79, 80, 119, 166
Procedure   ix, 55, 58, 64, 73, 122, 124, 126, 141, 167
Procedures   10, 20, 21, 25, 42, 84, 110, 138, 144, 146, 147, 151, 159, 161
  set   10, 138, 144, 146, 147
Profit   2, 3, 5, 8, 14, 26, 43, 89, 101, 103
Prohibition   71, 91
Project   35-37, 48, 49, 110-112
  special   109, 110
  improvement   48, 50
Proof, documented   155
Property   4, 7, 9, 13, 15, 18, 19, 29, 34, 40, 41, 52, 76, 82-85, 104, 105, 157
  common   13, 15, 20, 38, 39, 58, 69, 70, 73, 75-77
  community   13
  insurable
    Common Area   38
    Exclusive Common Area   39
Property Maintenance Code Ordinances   152
Property owners   15, 61-63, 101, 104
Property Owners Association   4, 8, 9, 14, 32, 33, 39, 40
Property
  personal   103, 129, 144

prices, residential   102
private   18, 19, 46
Proxy   12, 81, 86, 87, 108, 132, 133, 137
Purchase   32, 33, 40, 41, 77, 92, 102, 103, 140
Purchaser   33, 157

Q
Quorum   23, 27, 36, 45, 50, 75, 86, 87, 106, 115, 119-122, 128, 133, 134, 136, 142, 143

R
Recall   54, 82-87, 115, 146
  agreements   83, 84
  effort   83
Receipt   32, 33, 41, 68, 82, 116, 120, 135, 148, 159, 164-166
Receiver   27, 122
Receivership   122
Record
  date   136, 140
  parcel owner   134
Recorded document   14
Recordings   25, 40, 49, 53, 66, 70, 138, 140, 148, 168
Records, public   25, 86, 87
Regulations   5, 15, 16, 18, 30, 38, 46, 103, 105, 144, 154
Reimbursement   22, 34, 50, 52
Remedy   28, 51, 56
Remuneration   88
Repair   3, 12, 15, 17, 24, 30, 34, 38, 45, 46, 48, 50, 51, 102, 144, 169
Repairs   xv, 3, 11, 12, 17, 24, 30, 31, 34, 38, 39, 45, 46, 48, 50, 89, 90, 102, 155, 169, 170
Replace   3, 17, 45, 92,

176

102, 164
Replacement   38, 39, 46, 48, 84, 113, 114
 cost   38, 39
Report   147, 151, 154, 163
Requirements   29, 34, 37, 42, 43, 58, 86, 87, 120, 128, 135, 141, 166
 following   44, 70, 72, 110
Reserves   xvi, 31, 40, 41, 104, 109, 112-114, 142
Resign   107, 116, 139, 150, 151, 161
Resignations   xvi, 10, 115, 116, 121
 automatic   116
Resolutions   50, 54, 57, 59, 94, 119, 124, 131, 133, 143, 169
Restrictions   2, 3, 16, 27, 30-32, 38, 59-61, 76, 77, 96, 102, 103, 105, 106, 108, 109, 144, 149
Retaliation   90
Right   18, 29-31, 45, 56-59, 66, 67, 76, 78, 85, 87-89, 92, 119, 120, 136, 137, 142, 157
Risk   20, 22, 74
Road   3, 34
Robert's Rules of order   122, 170
Roof   3, 12, 30, 31, 45, 61, 62, 112, 154, 156
Rule   16, 72-76, 81, 90, 92, 95, 162

S
Sale   32, 33, 41, 52, 68, 128, 157, 167
Sanction   24, 55, 79
Screen   32, 153, 156
Servitude   13, 15, 16, 70
Showering   93, 94
Showers   17, 95, 96
Shutters   61, 62, 154

Signs   25, 63, 76, 77, 92, 97, 120, 125, 135, 170
Special assessment   50, 73, 109-113
Sprinkler system   21, 34, 112, 145
Standard   32, 35, 73, 92, 152, 159, 160
Stucco   3, 156
Subordination   52, 131
Supermajority   23, 24, 48, 49, 58, 69, 70, 124, 168

T
Tax   49, 91, 165
Term of office   24, 80, 119
Termination   40, 52, 53, 152
Termination Instrument   53
Title   2, 8, 29, 38, 39, 61, 91, 102, 103, 157
Training   6, 118, 140, 149, 150, 161
Transfer   37, 38, 52, 104, 157, 167
Tree removal   19, 46, 112
Trees   18, 19, 46, 113

U
Utility   29, 31, 145
Utopia   1, 3-8, 13-15, 17-20, 26-34, 37-41, 43-48, 50-54, 59-64, 101-103, 105, 107-109, 157-159, 168-170

V
Vacancies   27, 84, 115, 122, 142, 143, 146
Value   1, 22, 38, 61, 89, 102, 128, 169
Vested interest   155, 157
Violation

177

alleged   25, 67, 81, 90
of governing documents
   56, 68
intentional   91
second   24, 93, 94
Vote   23-25, 36, 37, 60, 61,
   64, 65, 69, 70, 75-78,
   83-87, 106-109, 115,
   116, 121, 123, 124, 133,
   134, 136-140, 142, 146,
   147
   affirmative   48-50, 115, 168
   approve   64
   authorizing   58
   counting   108, 138
   rejected   85
Voter, authorized   106
Voters, eligible   23, 138
Voting   xvi-xviii, 10, 21, 25,
   71, 74-76, 86, 106, 108,
   109, 115, 123, 125, 133,
   142, 164
   interests   12, 45, 119, 134
   total eligible   134, 135,
   164
   membership   8, 48, 49
   power   70, 71, 74, 81-83,
   87
   total   82

W
Wall   16, 31, 47, 93, 94, 107
Warning   24, 63, 92, 98, 116,
   125
Washing   3, 11, 112
Window   154, 155
Working   xv, 11, 22, 78, 91,
   96, 115, 132, 152, 153

* **This index was Created
with TExtract © Texyz 2007
a product of Texyz Indexing
Software – www.texyz.com**

178

ABOUT THE AUTHOR

Dr. David I. Goldenberg is an international business consultant. He specialized in quickly developing practical solutions to top management problems in business economics and corporate strategy. Before moving to Florida, he relaxed by teaching business economics and related subjects as an adjunct professor, primarily in off-campus evening MBA courses for Fairleigh Dickinson University. He earned an MBA from Columbia University and a Ph.D. in economics from the New School University.

Dr. Goldenberg has published two major books, a number of book-length reports for management and numerous articles. He's currently writing up some 40 humorous incidents from his career as a new book.

Besides writing, consulting and occasionally teaching or giving a presentation, Dr. Goldenberg serves as the Secretary of the Cyber Citizens for Justice, a Florida-based consumer alliance, and as the lead outside director of a startup firm.

Dave, as he prefers to be known, lives in a condominium community in Boynton Beach, Florida. He used to live in an HOA where he started and led the Documents Review Committee. E-mail him at SUNTZU3@GOLDENBERG.ORG or SUNTZU3@BELLSOUTH.NET.

OTHER WORKS BY THE AUTHOR

The Art of War 3: The Canons of Commerce, 1st Books Library, Bloomington, IN 2002

The U.S. Man-Made Fiber Industry: Its Structure and Organization since 1948, Praeger, Westport, CT 1992